MW01264561

100 Irresistible Recipes

PRESSURE

PURE

COOKING

COME ON... JUST COOK IT!

By Jennifer Lynn

Table of contents

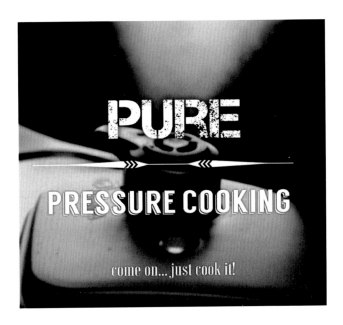

Pure Pressure Cooking Basics

1. **The cook time in the recipe is NOT the total time it will take to cook.** Your electric pressure cooker takes time to come to pressure, as well as release pressure. So, allow for at least 10 extra minutes of cooking time to prevent disappointing guests or family.

2. **You don't have to THAW frozen foods before cooking in your pressure cooker.** The whole purpose is convenience, right? Why spend minutes or even hours thawing something, when you can just toss it in and have the exact same flavorful taste? However, I would advise you to add a couple of minutes to your recipe if substituting for frozen.

3. **You can use dry beans and grains WITHOUT soaking first.** I would recommend that you briefly rinse them off under cold water to avoid sticking to the pot, but it is not completely necessary in some recipes.

4. **Double and triple check your venting knob before setting your cook time.** We've been there. Nothing worse that allowing

for your entire meal to "cook", only to realize it never actually came to pressure.

5. **Know what is meant by NATURAL pressure release (NPR) or QUICK RELEASE (QR).** NPR is when you literally do NOTHING once your timer goes off. You'll notice it changes to an L000, L001, etc. Allow it to count upwards however many minutes according to the recipe, and then open the vent knob when finished. QR is simply flipping your vent knob and immediately allowing the pressure to release. With either method, the pin will drop when ALL pressure has been released.

6. **ALWAYS keep at least 1 cup of liquid in your pot when cooking.** Some recipes will count for liquid being disbursed from meats or vegetables, which is why it might appear to be using less than the recommended amount of liquid.

7. **MANUAL pressure means A LOT of different things, so know your particular model of Instant Pot or pressure cooker.** With Instant Pot LUX models, manual is simply the "manual" button. With Instant Pot Duo, Ultra, Smart, & Max, the manual button says, "pressure cook". These are the various Instant Pots we used for these recipes, but keep in mind there are hundreds of electric pressure cookers. \

8. **You can use ANYTHING that is oven and dish-washer safe in you Instant Pot or pressure cooker.** Glass, silicone, aluminum, etc. Just make sure you read your labels closely!

9. **NEVER use your pressure cooker on or near the stovetop!** Don't smirk. Accidents DO happen, and knobs get bumped. Just don't.

10. **AVOID transporting your pressure cooker while AT pressure.** Again, accidents… pressure … just don't!

11. **ALWAYS have your inner pot inside your Instant Pot when cooking.** And NEVER put liquid or anything on the heating stone that's under it.

12. **Just because we used a particular model or size of Instant Pot, doesn't mean that yours can't make it.** It most certainly can. Whether you have a 3QT, 6QT, or an 8QT, all it means is how much you can fit in it. The cook time will be EXACTLY the same. These recipes were all crafted for the average 6QT Instant Pot, so just double or slash the ingredients in half if you have a different size.

BREAKFAST

Colossal Chocolate Chip Pancake

Ingredients

- 1 cup chocolate chips
- 2 cups flour
- 1 ½ cups milk
- 2 eggs
- 2 Tbsp sugar
- 1 Tbsp pure vanilla extract
- 3 tsp baking powder
- 1 tsp. salt
- nonstick cooking spray
- butter (for serving)
- favorite syrup for serving (I used maple in the picture, but strawberry is amazing with this topping combo.)
- your favorite toppings (GET CREATIVE!!)
- aluminum foil

To Prepare:

1) In a large bowl, mix all your ingredients until everything is blended smoothly.

2) I used an 8" push pan (but a spring form pan also works great) for this. Spray the bottom and sides well with nonstick cooking spray.

3) Pour batter into pan and cover with aluminum foil. If you don't have handles on your trivet, you will want to make a sling out of foil to remove your push pan.

4) Add 2 cups water to pressure pot and place trivet in pot. Lower push pan to rest on trivet. Close and seal the lid. Cook on manual HIGH pressure for 50 minutes. Quick release pressure.

5) Remove push pan from the pot and uncover. Check pancake with a toothpick to make sure it is done (cook for extra 5 minutes if needed). Add your favorite toppings! Serve & ENJOY!

Perfect Pancake Bites

Ingredients

- 1 cup flour
- 1 egg
- 1 Tbsp pure vanilla extract
- ½ Tbsp sugar
- 1 tsp baking powder
- 1/8 tsp salt
- ¾ cup milk
- butter
- blueberries (I substituted chocolate chips in half)
- maple syrup (or blueberry?!)
- aluminum foil

To Prepare:

1) In a mixing bowl, combine all the ingredients (except for blueberries, syrup, or butter!) Mix until smooth.

2) Very gently stir in blueberries.

3) Carefully pour the batter into the silicone egg molds (pictured in the back of book). Then cover the mold with aluminum foil to ensure no water gets inside.

4) Add 1 ½ cups water to pressure pot and set trivet inside. Lower silicone mold onto trivet. Close & seal lid.

5) Cook on manual HIGH pressure for 5 minutes. Allow for 3 minutes of Normal Pressure Release and then Quick Release the remaining pressure.

6) Open lid and remove your mold. Uncover the foil, place a plate on top of the mold and then flip it over to remove your pancake bites. Top with butter and syrup. ENJOY!

Pure Pressure Breakfast Scramble

Ingredients

- 2 cups chopped ham (or sausage/bacon/BOTH)
- 8 eggs
- ½ cup milk
- 2 cups shredded cheddar
- 1 medium onion, diced
- 1 green pepper, diced
- 2 cups hash browns (unfrozen)
- 1 tsp salt
- 1 tsp pepper
- Nonstick cooking spray

To Prepare:

1) Press sauté mode to preheat your pressure pot.

2) In a separate mixing bowl, whisk 8 eggs, ½ cup milk, 1 tsp salt & pepper together.

3) Spray your pressure pot with nonstick cooking spray. Add ham (or any meat) to the pot, along with green pepper and onion. Cook until lightly browned. Turn off pot.

4) Spread meat mixture evenly around bottom of pot. Apply hash browns as your next layer and again, spread evenly.

5) Last, evenly pour your egg-mixture over the hash browns to create the final layer.

6) Close and seal lid. Cook on manual HIGH pressure for 12 minutes. Allow for a 5-minute Natural Pressure Release and Quick Release any remaining pressure.

7) Open lid and "fluff" your scramble with a fork or spoon. Serve with buttery toast and ENJOY!

Country Boy Biscuits & Gravy

Ingredients

- 1 can of your favorite refrigerated biscuits (I prefer good ole Grands!)
- 1lb ground Italian sausage
- 1Tbsp butter
- 1 cup chicken broth
- ½ cup flour
- 3 cups milk
- ½ tsp salt
- ½ tsp pepper
- Non-stick cooking spray
- Aluminum foil

To Prepare:

1) Spray silicone egg-bite mold (see back of book for picture) with non-stick cooking spray. Roll each biscuit into a small ball and place throughout your egg-bite mold. Cover with aluminum foil.

2) Press Sauté mode on your pot to preheat it. In your pressure pot, add butter, sausage, salt& pepper. Cook until sausage is fully browned.

3) Without draining the grease, add in 1cup of chicken both to the pressure pot. (Make sure to deglaze your pot here if necessary).

4) Place your egg-bite mold onto your trivet, and lower onto the top of the sausage mixture. Close & seal lid.

5) Cook on manual HIGH pressure for 10 minutes.

6) Before timer is up, in a separate mixing bowl, whisk together ½ cup flour and 3 cups milk until fully dissolved.

7) Quick release pressure when timer is up. Remove biscuits & trivet.

8) Now, add your milk mixture to the pressure pot and press Sauté. Continue to stir until gravy thickens.

(Don't overcook, it will thicken as it cools.)

9) Cut up biscuits however you prefer (I slice each bite into thirds) and serve with gravy over top. ENJOY!!

PRO TIP: Use HOT sausage and ¼ cup Franks red hot sauce for a "Spicy" Country Boy

Pure Pressure Omelette Casserole

Ingredients

- 1 cup shredded cheddar cheese
- 1 cup mushrooms diced
- 1/2 green pepper, diced
- 1/2 red pepper, diced
- 1 cup shredded hash browns (I used unfrozen, but frozen work too)
- 6 eggs
- 1/2 cup milk or cream
- Cooked meat (optional)
- Non-stick cooking spray
- Aluminum foil
- Parsley (optional)

To Prepare:

1) Spray spring form pan with non-stick cooking spray. (Or ramekins for individual topping mini omelettes)

2) Place 1/4 cup shredded cheddar in the bottom of the spring form pan.

3) In a mixing-bowl, whisk the eggs, then add the milk and 1/4 cup shredded cheddar. Mix-well.

4) Mix in the meat, mushrooms, green peppers, red peppers, and hash browns.

5) Pour egg mixture over shredded cheese in the spring form pan. Cover with aluminum foil and make a foil sling.

6) Add 2 cup of water and trivet to the pressure pot. Place spring form pan on the trivet and close the lid.

7) Cook on manual HIGH pressure for 10 minutes. Allow for a 5-minute Natural Pressure Release, and then Quick Release any remaining pressure.

8) Open lid and remove pan. Remove aluminum foil and top with remaining cheese. Serve & Enjoy!!

PRO TIP: Place sausage gravy in a separate cooking dish and cover with foil. Cook right along with your Omelette. Serve over top!

Pure Pressure English Muffins

Ingredients

- As many eggs as desired
- Favorite cooked breakfast meat (or sauté meat beforehand)
- Sliced cheddar cheese
- English muffins
- Salt
- Pepper
- Non-stick cooking spray

To Prepare:

1) Spray ramekins with non-stick cooking spray.

2) Designate 1 ramekin for your favorite meat.

3) Place 1 egg per ramekin and sprinkle with a pinch of salt and pepper (1 sandwich).

4) Place English muffins in toaster and start it.

5) Add 1 cup water and trivet to pressure pot. Place ramekins on trivet and close lid.

6) Cook on manual HIGH pressure for 3 minutes. (2 minutes if you want a runny yolk). Quick release the pressure.

7) Open lid and remove ramekins. Stack your eggs and meat on cooked English muffin and top with a slice of cheddar cheese. ENJOY!!

Compelling Cinnamon Rolls

Ingredients

Filling

- 3/4 cup light brown sugar packed
- 6 Tbsp white sugar
- 2 tsp cinnamon
- 1/8 tsp ground cloves
- 1/8 tsp salt
- 1 Tbsp butter melted

Rolls

- 1 1/4 cup buttermilk
- 2 1/2 cups flour (plus a little extra to work with)
- 1 1/4 tsp baking powder
- 1/2 tsp baking soda
- 1/2 tsp salt
- 7 Tbsp butter melted

Icing

- 2 Tbsp cream cheese softened
- 2 1/2 Tbsp milk
- 1 1/2 cups powdered sugar

Misc.

- Aluminum foil
- Non-stick cooking spray

To Prepare:

1) In a mixing bowl, whisk together the light brown sugar, 4 Tbsp white sugar, cinnamon, cloves, and salt. Then, add in melted butter and mix until it is a paste.

2) Spray 7" spring form pan with non-stick cooking spray.

3) In a large bowl, whisk together the flour, remaining 2 Tbsp white sugar, baking powder, baking soda, and 1/2 tsp salt.

4) In a separate cup, mix 2 Tbsp melted butter with the 1 ¼ cup buttermilk.

5) Add buttermilk mixture to the flour and other dry ingredients and mix until it has started to form dough.

6) Pour your dough onto a floured surface and knead until the dough becomes smooth dough.

7) Roll the cinnamon roll dough into a rectangle. Then, brush the dough with 2 Tbsp melted butter.

8) Sprinkle the filling onto the dough and make sure to leave 1/4 inch of space around the edges.

9) Roll the dough lengthwise until it resembles a log. Pinch the seams along the edge and on the ends so they stick.

10) Cut the log into 6 equal pieces. Place one piece in the center of your spring form pan and the remaining 5 around the center cinnamon roll.

11) Brush the tops of the rolls with the remaining 2 tablespoons melted butter. Cover pan with aluminum foil and make a foil sling.

12) Add 2 cups water and trivet to your pressure pot.

13) Lower your spring form pan into your pressure pot.

14) Close lid and seal. Cook on manual HIGH pressure for 23 minutes. Allow 15 minutes for Natural Pressure Release. Quick release any remaining steam.

15) Open lid and gently remove the pan using your foil sling. Remove aluminum foil and pour icing directly on top. Allow 10 minutes to cool. Serve & ENJOY!

To make the icing: Mix together softened cream cheese and 2 Tbsp milk. Whisk in the powdered sugar until smooth.

Pure Pressure Breakfast Quinoa

Ingredients

• 1 1/2 cups uncooked quinoa (rinse well to avoid sticking)

• 2 Tbsp maple syrup

• 1/2 tsp vanilla

• 1/4 tsp ground cinnamon

• ½ tsp salt

• Milk, fresh berries, honey, or sliced almonds for toppings (optional)

To Prepare:

1) Add all ingredients (except for optional) to your pressure pot.

2) Close lid and seal. Cook on manual HIGH pressure for 1 minute. Allow for a 10-minute Natural Pressure Release, then Quick Release remaining steam.

3) Open lid and fluff Quinoa with a fork or spoon. Scoop into bowl and serve with your favorite combination of milk, berries, honey, or almonds! ENJOY!

Mini-Cini Bites

Ingredients

Dough

- 3/4 cup light brown sugar, packed
- 6 Tbsp white sugar
- 2 tsp cinnamon
- 1/8 tsp ground cloves
- 1/8 tsp salt
- 1 Tbsp butter melted
- 1 1/4 cup buttermilk
- 2 1/2 cups flour (plus a little extra to work with)
- 1 1/4 tsp baking powder
- 1/2 tsp baking soda
- 1/2 tsp salt
- 7 Tbsp butter melted

Icing

- 2 Tbsp cream cheese softened
- 2 1/2 Tbsp milk
- 1 1/2 cups powdered sugar

Misc.

- Aluminum foil
- Non-stick cooking spray
- Silicone Egg-bite mold (see back of book)

To Prepare:

1) In a mixing bowl, whisk together the light brown sugar, 4 Tbsp white sugar, cinnamon, cloves, and salt. Then, add in melted butter and mix until it is a paste.

2) Spray egg-bite mold with non-stick cooking spray.

3) In a large bowl, whisk together the flour, remaining 2

Tbsp white sugar, baking powder, baking soda, and 1/2 tsp salt.

4) In a separate cup, mix 2 Tbsp melted butter with the 1 ¼ cup buttermilk.

5) Add buttermilk mixture to the flour and other dry ingredients and mix until it has started to form dough.

6) Pour your dough onto a floured surface and knead until the dough becomes smooth dough.

7) Roll the cinnamon roll dough into a rectangle. Then, brush the dough with 2 Tbsp melted butter.

8) Sprinkle the filling onto the dough and make sure to leave 1/4 inch of space around the edges.

9) Roll the dough lengthwise until it resembles a log. Pinch the seams along the edge and on the ends so they stick.

10) Cut the log into 7 pieces. Roll each individual piece into a ball and place into each section of your egg-bite mold. Then, cover your mold with aluminum foil.

11) Add 2 cups water and trivet to your pressure pot. Cook on manual HIGH pressure for 20 minutes. Allow for a 10-minute Natural Pressure Release, then Quick Release any remaining steam.

To make the icing:

1) Mix together softened cream cheese and 2 Tbsp milk. Whisk in the powdered sugar until smooth.

2) Open lid and remove egg-bite mold. Remove aluminum foil. Drizzle with packaged icing or save for dipping! Serve & ENJOY!

Fantastic Frittatas

Ingredients

- 8 eggs
- ½ cup plain Greek yogurt
- 1 tsp salt
- 1 tsp pepper
- 1tsp parsley
- 1 cup asparagus, chopped
- ½ cup spinach, chopped
- Non-stick cooking spray
- Aluminum foil

To Prepare:

1) In a mixing bowl, combine 8 eggs, ½ cup Greek yogurt, salt & pepper.

2) Once blended, add in chopped asparagus and spinach.

3) Spray non-stick cooking spray into silicone egg-bite molds (see back of book) and pour egg mixture to the top of each mold. Cover with aluminum foil.

4) Add 2 cups water and trivet to your pressure pot. Set egg-bite mold on trivet.

5) Close and seal lid. Cook on manual HIGH pressure for 5 minutes. Quick Release the pressure when done.

6) Open lid, uncover and remove frittatas from the mold. Serve with hot sauce and ENJOY!

Fluffy Fried Eggs

Ingredients

- Eggs (as many as desired)
- Salt
- Pepper
- Non-stick cooking spray

To Prepare:

1) Spray ramekins with non-stick cooking spray.

2) Crack each egg into separate ramekin and top with a pinch of salt & pepper.

3) Add 1 cup water and trivet to your pressure pot. Place ramekins on trivet.

4) Close and seal lid. Cook on manual HIGH pressure for 2 minutes for a little runnier yolk, or 3 minutes for a harder yolk. Quick Release the pressure when done.

5) Serve with buttery toast and ENJOY!

SOUPS

Hearty Chicken & Cheese Tortellini Soup

Ingredients

- 3 large boneless chicken breasts (or 4 small)
- 3 carrots, chopped
- 3 stalks celery, chopped
- 1 large onion, chopped
- 2 cloves of garlic (or 1 Tbsp garlic powder)
- 48oz chicken broth
- 2 Tbsp butter
- 1 Tbsp Italian seasoning
- 1 Tbsp parsley
- 1 tsp salt
- 1 tsp pepper
- 1 (20oz) bag of cheese Tortellini (Frozen works perfectly!)
- Parmesan cheese to top (Optional)

To Prepare:

1) Place all your ingredients, except for the Tortellini and about 2 cups of broth, into the pot. Give it a good stir. Close and seal the lid. Cook on manual HIGH pressure for 10 minutes. Quick release the pressure.

2) Open the lid and remove chicken breasts.

3) While you are shredding your chicken, add the bag of Tortellini to the pot and close the lid. Cook on manual HIGH pressure for 3 minutes. Quick release the pressure. (Watch for hot broth and cover with paper towel if needed.)

4) Open the lid. Add in your shredded chicken and remaining 2 cups of chicken broth. Give it a good stir. Serve with warm crusty bread or crackers and ENJOY!

Pure Creamy Tortellini Soup

Ingredients

• 1lb ground Italian sausage

• 1 large white onion

• 2 large carrots

• 2 stalks celery

• 4 cloves of garlic (or 1Tbsp garlic powder)

• 1 Tbsp Italian seasoning

• 2 tsp salt

• 2 tsp pepper

• 2 tsp chicken bouillon

• 6 cups chicken broth

• ¼ cup cornstarch mixed/dissolved in ¼ cup water

• 5 cups Half-and-Half (you can also use regular milk or heavy cream)

• 1 12oz pack of your favorite Tortellini (I use fresh Cheese Stuffed Tortellini, add 1-2 minutes if using frozen)

• 5 cups baby spinach

• Parmesan Cheese to top the soup

To Prepare:

1) Brown sausage, onion, carrots, celery, garlic, Italian seasoning, chicken bouillon powder, salt & pepper into your pressure cooker pot using the Sauté function. (at least a 6qt size recommended)

2) Add chicken broth, tortellini, baby spinach, and cornstarch/water mixture into the pot and scrape bottom of pressure cooker pot if needed.

3) Close & Seal pressure cooker, set timer to 3 minutes of High pressure using the Manual setting and LET IT COOK!

4) Allow up to 10 minutes of normal pressure release and then flip to quick release and uncover. (You can skip the 10-minute wait but be very careful of the steam)

5) Add 5 cups of Half-and-Half and press Sauté function, allowing soup to warm for 2 more minutes. Sprinkle soup with as much parmesan cheese as desired and ENJOY!

Pure Pressure Creamy Cheeseburger Soup

Ingredients

- 1lb. ground beef
- 1 white onion
- 1 tsp garlic (or garlic powder)
- 2 celery stalks
- 1 carrot, julienned.
- 5 medium potatoes, (I prefer Russet) peeled and chopped.
- 1 tsp salt
- 1 tsp pepper
- 1 lb. Velveeta cheese, cubed. (for various flavors try Velveeta Pepper jack, Jalapeno, or Queso!!)
- 3 cups chicken broth
- 1 Tbsp parsley
- 2 cups milk
- ¼ cup flour
- ½ cup sour cream

To Prepare:

1) Brown beef, onion, celery, carrots, garlic, salt & pepper on Sauté mode in pressure pot until beef is fully browned.

2) Add in broth, parsley and potatoes and scrape any necessary remains from bottom of pot.

3) Seal and set pressure cooker to 5 minutes HIGH pressure. Quick release the pressure when finished.

4) In a small bowl, whisk 2 cups milk and ¼ cup flour until smooth. Open lid and add in milk mixture, Velveeta cheese, and ½ cup sour cream. Stir until cheese is melted. ENJOY!!

Pure Creamy Broccoli and Cheddar Cheese Soup

Ingredients

- 1 lb. Broccoli, chopped
- 1 white onion
- 2 carrots, julienned
- 2 cloves of garlic (or 1 Tbsp garlic powder)
- ¼ cup flour
- 3 Tbsp butter
- 4 cups chicken broth
- 1 tsp mustard powder
- ¼ tsp nutmeg
- 1 tsp salt
- 1 tsp pepper
- 1 cup heavy cream
- 3 cups sharp cheddar cheese (try substituting half cheese with Gouda or Monterey Jack for an extra creamy texture)

To Prepare:

1) Add butter, onion, and carrots to your pressure pot and Sauté until it starts to turn light brown.

2) Mix in garlic and flour and cook for 1 minute until the flour starts to get lumpy. Quickly add in broth and whisk until the lumps are dissolved.

3) Add in broccoli, mustard powder, nutmeg, salt & pepper and seal the lid. Set pot to HIGH pressure and allow to cook for 7 minutes, then do a quick release.

4) Open the lid and mix in the cheese and heavy cream. Continue to stir until cheese is fully melted. Serve in your favorite bread bowl and ENJOY!

Pure Creamy Chicken & Wild Rice Soup

Ingredients

• 2 boneless chicken breasts (If smaller, add an extra)

• 1 box of wild rice (I prefer the 4.3oz box of Rice-A-Roni Wild Rice as it contains a delicious seasoning packet)

6 cups chicken broth

• 1 clove of garlic (or 1 tsp garlic powder)

• 1 tsp basil

• 1 tsp oregano

• 1 tsp salt

• 1 tsp pepper

• 1 cup heavy cream (or half-n-half)

• 2 large carrots, chopped

• 2 stalks celery, chopped

• 1 onion, chopped

• 2 Tbsp olive/vegetable oil

• 2 Tbsp cornstarch

To Prepare:

1) Add 2 Tbsp oil, vegetables, clove of garlic, salt & pepper to your pressure pot and cook until vegetables are brown using the "Sauté" mode on your cooker.

2) Add chicken, wild rice (and seasoning if using Rice-A-Roni), broth, 1 tsp basil, & 1 tsp oregano into the pot. Cook on HIGH pressure for 15 minutes, or if using frozen chicken, cook for 30 minutes. Quick release your pressure.

3) Remove chicken and shred (or you can do it right in the pot for less of a mess) Add back to the pot and put your pot on "Sauté" mode.

4) Whisk 1 cup of broth mixture with 2tbs cornstarch in a separate bowl until fully dissolved and then add to soup.

5) Pour in 1 cup heavy cream and continue to sauté until soup thickens to your preference. DO NOT over sauté, as your soup will continue to thicken as it cools. SERVE & ENJOY!!!

Loaded Cauliflower & Potato Soup

Ingredients

- 1lb gold potatoes, cubed
- 1 medium head of cauliflower, remove leaves and cut into chunks
- 1/2 lb. bacon, chopped
- 4 cloves of garlic, minced
- 4 cups chicken broth
- 1 cup whole milk
- ½ tsp. pepper
- ½ tsp salt
- 2 cups grated cheddar cheese (plus extra for topping)
- Green onion (optional)

To Prepare:

1) Set pressure pot to sauté mode. Add in bacon and garlic. Cook for 3-4 minutes until bacon is done. Remove a couple pieces for topping, crumble the rest and leave in the pot.

2) Add in the peeled potatoes, chopped cauliflower and chicken stock. Deglaze your pot if necessary.

3) Close lid and seal. Cook on manual HIGH pressure for 10 minutes. Allow for a 10-minute Natural Pressure Release, then Quick Release any remaining steam.

4) Open lid and add in the milk and 2 cups cheese. Mash the potatoes and cauliflower with a potato masher or blender until you like the consistency. Add more broth if desired.

5) Serve in a bowl and top with extra cheddar cheese, bacon crumbles, and green onion! ENJOY!

Fiesta Chicken Tortilla Soup

Ingredients

- 2 (14ozz) cans diced tomatoes
- 3 boneless chicken breasts
- 1 onion, diced
- 1 (4oz.) can of diced green chiles
- 1/2 cup chicken broth
- 2 cloves of garlic, minced
- 1 tsp ground cumin
- 1 tsp salt
- 1 tsp pepper
- 4 Corn tortillas cut into 1/4-inch strips
- 2 Tbsp cilantro, chopped
- 1/2 cup shredded Monterey Jack cheese
- 1 avocado, diced and tossed with lime juice
- Lime wedges

To Prepare:

1) Add tomatoes, chicken, chiles, broth, onion, garlic, cumin, salt and pepper into pressure pot and stir well.

2) Close lid and cook on manual HIGH pressure for 9 minutes. Allow for a 10-minute Natural Pressure Release and Quick Release any remaining steam.

3) Open lid and remove chicken to a plate for shredding. Once shredded, add back to the pot.

4) Press Sauté; add tortillas and cilantro to soup. Cook and stir 2 minutes or until heated through. Top with cheese, avocado and squeeze of lime juice.

5) Serve immediately. ENJOY!!

Pure Pressure Beefy Crunch Soup

Ingredients

- 1lb ground beef
- 1 Tbsp olive oil
- 1 tsp salt
- 1 tsp pepper
- 2 Tbsp taco seasoning (I used Taco Bell's here, of course!)
- 1 (14.5 oz.) can of fire roasted diced tomatoes
- 3 cups milk
- 1 cup Spanish rice
- 2 cups chicken broth
- 1 cup shredded cheddar cheese (plus extra for topping)
- Sour cream for topping (optional)
- Crushed tortilla chips for topping (use Flaming Hot Fritos for true Beefy Crunch spice!)

To Prepare:

1) Press sauté mode on your pressure pot. When hot, add 1 Tbsp olive oil, ground beef, salt & pepper. Cook until burger is lightly browned.

2) Add in diced tomatoes, taco seasoning, Spanish rice, and chicken broth. Make sure to deglaze your pot if necessary.

3) Close and seal lid. Cook on manual HIGH pressure for 8 minutes. Allow for a 5-minute Natural Pressure Release and then Quick Release the remaining steam.

4) Open lid and stir in 3 cups milk and 1 cup shredded cheddar cheese. Use sauté mode to bring to heat and melt the cheese.

5) Top with more cheese, sour cream, and Flaming Hot Fritos!! ENJOY!!!

Pure *LOADED* Baked Potato Soup

Ingredients

- 2 Tbsp butter
- 1 onion, chopped
- 6 medium potatoes, peeled and cubed
- 2 (14 oz.) cans chicken broth
- 1 tsp salt
- 1 tsp pepper
- 1/8 tsp crushed red pepper
- 2 Tbsp parsley
- 2 Tbsp corn starch
- 3 oz. of cream cheese, cubed
- 1 cup shredded cheddar cheese (extra to garnish)
- 2 cups heavy cream
- 6 slices of crisp-cooked bacon, crumbled
- Green onion to garnish (optional)

To Prepare:

1) Press sauté mode on your pressure pot. When hot, add 2 Tbsp butter and chopped onion. Sauté until onion is lightly browned.

2) Add 2 cans chicken broth, 1/8 tsp red pepper, 2 Tsp parsley, salt & pepper to the pot. Give it a good stir.

3) Place steamer basket (see back of book) into pot and place your cubed potatoes in it.

4) Close and seal lid. Cook on manual HIGH pressure for 4 minutes. Allow for a 5-minute Natural Pressure Release and then Quick Release remaining steam.

5) Open lid to remove potatoes and steam rack. Press sauté mode again on your pressure pot.

6) In a separate mixing bowl, whisk 2 Tbsp corn starch and 2

Tbsp water until dissolved. Then, slowly add this to your soup and stir it constantly.

7) Add 3oz. of cream cheese and 1 cup shredded cheddar cheese and stir until melted.

8) Then, add back your potatoes and remaining ingredients. Bring to a heat but not to a boil. Serve with extra cheese and green onion. ENJOY!!

LUNCH/DINNER

Pure Pressure Orange Chicken and Rice

Ingredients

- 3-4 Boneless Chicken Breasts
- ¾ BBQ Sauce (Darker sauce recommended)
- 1 tsp cornstarch
- 1 cup orange marmalade
- 2 cloves of garlic (or 1 Tbsp garlic powder)
- ½ tsp minced ginger
- ½ tsp red chili flakes
- 1 tsp salt
- 1 tsp pepper
- 2 Tbsp soy sauce
- Green onions, chopped
- Your favorite rice (I use White)

To Prepare:

1) Cut chicken into good bite sized pieces and add into pressure pot. Cover with BBQ, soy sauce, garlic, ginger, red chili flakes, salt & pepper. Set cooker to HIGH pressure and allow it to cook for 4 minutes. Quick release when done.

2) Either remove chicken from pot (or BBQ) and whisk in cornstarch. You don't want to whisk your chicken, or it will shred.

3) Add 1 cup orange marmalade to sauce and stir well.

4) Once fully mixed, add chicken back to pot and Sauté everything until sauce starts to thicken. Don't overdo it, you will want to allow this to cool off for a few minutes which will also thicken your sauce.

5) Serve over your favorite rice dish and top with green onions. ENJOY!!

Pure Pressure Creamy Chicken Spaghetti

Ingredients

- 4 Boneless Chicken Breasts
- 2 cans of Rotel diced tomatoes & green chilies (10oz)
- 3 cups chicken broth
- 1 large white onion
- 1 cup/can of mushrooms
- 1 large green pepper, chopped
- 1 tsp salt
- 1 tsp pepper
- 1 pack Hidden Valley Ranch Dressing
- 1 tsp garlic
- 2 tsp paprika
- 16 oz. of your favorite thin spaghetti
- 8oz. cream cheese (one block)
- 4 cups shredded cheddar cheese

To Prepare:

1) Add chicken broth, boneless chicken breasts, ranch dressing, garlic, paprika, salt & pepper into the pot and set to HIGH pressure for 12 minutes. Allow at least 5 minutes of normal pressure release if you can. (If not, just be very careful!)

2) Open lid, add onion, green pepper, spaghetti noodles, & Rotel into the pot and re-seal the lid. Set timer to HIGH pressure for 3 minutes and quick release when finished.

3) Again, open the lid, and this time you will add the cream cheese and shredded cheddar cheese to the pot. Hit Sauté mode and cook until cheese is fully melted. ENJOY!

Pure Pressure Pizza Pasta

Ingredients

- 1 lb. ground Italian sausage
- 1 cup pizza sauce
- 2 cups spaghetti sauce
- 3 ½ cups water
- 1 cup mozzarella
- 1 cup green peppers
- 1 cup mushrooms
- 1 white onion
- 1 cup pepperoni
- 1lb. of your favorite pasta (I prefer cavatappi)
- 1 clove of garlic (or 1 tsp garlic powder)
- 1 tsp Italian seasoning
- 1 tsp salt
- 1 tsp pepper
- 1 Tbsp butter

To Prepare:

1) Add butter, garlic, Italian seasoning, sausage, onion, green pepper, mushrooms, salt & pepper into the pot and hit Sauté mode. Cook until sausage is fully browned.

2) Add both sauces, pasta, and water to the pot. Set to cook on HIGH pressure for 5 minutes and the quick release the steam.

3) Open lid, mix in half of the cheese and half of the pepperoni until cheese is fully melted.

4) Sprinkle remaining cheese and top with pepperoni. Set pressure cooker to WARM and replace the lid until the cheese on top has melted. SERVE & ENJOY!

Irresistibly Creamy Mac N' Cheese

Ingredients

- 1lb. of your favorite macaroni pasta (I prefer elbows or again, Cavatappi!)

- 4 cups water

- 4 Tbsp butter

- 1 tsp salt

- 1 tsp pepper

- 1 tsp ground mustard

- 1 can evaporated milk (5oz)

- 6 cups Velveeta cheese, shredded or cut into small cubes (6 cups are 3/4ths of the standard 32. oz block of Velveeta)

To Prepare:

1) Add water, macaroni, butter, ground mustard, salt & pepper into the pressure pot and close the lid. Set cooker to HIGH pressure and allow to cook for 4 minutes. Quick release the pressure.

2) Open the lid, stir in the evaporated milk and cheese. Hit Sauté mode on your pressure cooker and cook until cheese is fully melted. (Pro tip: Remove Mac N' Cheese from pot, place in baking dish and broil for 2-3 minutes) SERVE & ENJOY!!

Pure Mouth-Watering Lasagna

Ingredients

- 1lb ground Italian sausage
- 2 cloves of garlic (or 2 tsp garlic powder)
- 1 tsp salt
- 1 tsp pepper
- 2 tsp Italian seasoning
- ¼ cup parsley
- 1 tsp oregano
- ½ cup ricotta cheese
- ½ cup cottage cheese
- 1 cup shredded mozzarella
- 1 cup shredded/grated parmesan
- 3 cups of your favorite marinara sauce (The kids enjoy the Bertolli brand)
- 1 egg
- 1 box no-boil lasagna noodles

To Prepare:

1) Using Sauté mode, add ground Italian sausage, ½ tsp Italian seasoning, 1 clove of garlic (or 1 tsp powder), 1 tsp salt and 1 tsp pepper to the pot and cook until fully browned. Drain grease, clean pot, then add 1 ½ cups water and trivet to the bottom of pot.

2) In a separate bowl, mix together ½ cup ricotta cheese, ½ cup cottage cheese, ¼ cup parsley, ½ cup mozzarella, ½ cup parmesan, 1 ½ tsp Italian seasoning, 1 tsp oregano, and 1 egg until fully mixed, then set aside.

3) In a 7" springform pan (See back of the book), start a layer with your lasagna noodles by breaking them to perfectly fit the bottom of your pan.

4) Next, add 1cup marinara to the top of the noodles and spread around evenly.

5) Then, spread ½ of your ground Italian sausage on top of the sauce and spread evenly.

6) Finally, finish the first layer off by spreading ½ of the cheese mixture evenly over the sausage layer.

7) Repeat steps 3 through 6.

8) For the final layer, cover the cheese sauce with more lasagna noodles, then top noodles with remaining ½ cup mozzarella and ½ cup parmesan cheese.

9) Cover springform pan with aluminum foil and place on trivet inside the pot. (If your trivet doesn't have handles you will want to make an aluminum foil sling to hoist pan back out when finished.

10) Close the lid and seal your pot. Set to cook on manual HIGH pressure for 24 minutes. When timer beeps, allow it to do a Natural Pressure Release (do nothing) for 15 minutes. Quick release any remaining pressure.

11) This step is not 100% necessary, but I like to place the lasagna on a baking pan and broil until cheese is perfect (in my eyes) on top! SERVE & ENJOY!!

Sweet & Garlicky Chicken

Ingredients

- 4 chicken thighs (or boneless breasts work great!)
- 4 cloves of garlic
- ¼ cup parsley
- 1 tsp salt
- 1 tsp pepper
- 1 Tbsp vegetable oil
- ¼ cup honey
- 1 Tbsp brown sugar
- 1/8 cup soy sauce
- ¼ cup chicken broth (water can be used if needed)
- 1 tsp cayenne pepper

To Prepare:

1) In a mixing bowl, combine ¼ cup honey, 1 Tbsp brown sugar, 1/8 cup soy sauce, ¼ cup broth (or water), and 1 tsp cayenne pepper. Mix until everything is dissolved.

2) Preheat your pot using Sauté mode. While that is heating, season the chicken with salt & pepper. After the pot is hot, add cooking oil, garlic and chicken. Sear your chicken until it is brown on both sides and once it is, cover the chicken with the sauce you made.

3) Close the lid. Cook on manual HIGH pressure for 10 minutes. (I would only cook for 8 minutes if using boneless breasts).

4) Allow for a 5-minute Normal Pressure Release and then quick release any remaining pressure. Top with parsley, then SERVE & ENJOY!!

PRO TIP: Cut boneless chicken breasts into chunks and serve over egg fried/white rice for a tasty Asian cuisine.

Red Hot Ranch Pasta Bake

Ingredients

• 2 large boneless chicken breasts

• 1 cup Hidden Valley Ranch dressing

• 2 cups of your favorite pasta (16oz box., I prefer penne noodles for this recipe!)

• ½ cup Frank's Red-Hot Sauce

• 1 Tbsp butter

• 1 tsp salt

• 1 tsp pepper

• 1 cup cream cheese (8oz container)

• ½ cup shredded Mexican-style cheese

• 3 cups water

• Bacon bits to top (or fresh bacon. YUM!)

To Prepare:

1) Add chicken, 1 Tbsp butter, ¼ cup Frank's Red Hot, and 1 cup water to the pot and close the lid. Cook on manual HIGH pressure for 14 minutes (I would do 25 minutes if breasts are frozen) Quick release the pressure.

2) Open lid and shred chicken inside the pot (hand mixer works very well). Add 1 cup cream cheese, 1 cup ranch, and ¼ cup Frank's Red Hot to the chicken and stir until mixed well.

3) Add 2 cups pasta and 2 cups water to the pot, give it a good stir, and close the lid. Cook on manual HIGH pressure for 4 minutes. Quick release when timer beeps.

4) Open lid, mix everything up very well, and pour into baking dish. Cover with ½ cup shredded Mexican cheese and top with Bacon. Broil until desired. SERVE & ENJOY

Pure Addicting "Crack" Chicken Sandwiches

Ingredients

- 3 large boneless chicken breasts
- ½ lb. chopped bacon (pre-cooked OK for faster alternative)
- 1 packet of dry Hidden Valley Ranch mix
- 1 cup chicken broth
- 1 cup or 8oz container of cream cheese
- 1 Tbsp cornstarch
- 1 tsp salt
- 1 tsp pepper
- 1 cup shredded cheddar
- ¼ cup green onions
- Bag of your favorite buns/rolls (I prefer Kaiser or a toasted Hoagie bun!)

To Prepare:

1) Preheat cooker using Sauté function. Once hot, add chopped bacon and fully cook.

2) Add 1 cup chicken broth to the pot and deglaze your pot by scraping any remaining bits from the bottom. This is VERY important, or your pot won't come to pressure.

3) Mix in Hidden Valley Ranch packet. Add chicken breasts to the pot and top them with 1 cup of cream cheese.

4) Close & Seal the lid. Cook on manual HIGH pressure for 14 minutes. (25 minutes for frozen breasts) Allow for a 5-minute Natural Pressure Release.

5) Open lid, add 1 Tbsp cornstarch to the pot and use a hand mixer to shred the chicken and to mix your ingredients well. (If you don't have a hand mixer, remove chicken from pot and shred with a fork)

6) Stir in 1cup of shredded cheddar cheese and top with green onions. Place on your favorite bun or roll and ENJOY!!!

**PRO TIP: You can also serve this in a bowl with chips or crackers as a delicious appetizer!

Creamy Boneless Pork Chops & Rice

Ingredients

- 3-4 Boneless pork chops
- 1 medium onion, chopped
- 1 cup mushrooms
- 3 cups chicken broth
- 1 can cream of mushroom soup
- 1 tbsp olive oil
- 1 tsp salt
- 1 tsp pepper
- 1 tsp garlic powder

To Prepare:

1) Press "sauté" to heat your pot. Season pork chops with garlic powder, salt & pepper. Add 1Tbsp olive oil to the pot, followed by the pork chops. Cook until lightly browned on each side.

2) Remove pork chops from the pot. Add 1 cup chicken broth and deglaze your pot by scraping any remains from the bottom.

3) Add all the remaining ingredients (including the pork chops) back into the pot and give it a good stir.

4) Close and seal lid. Set to cook on manual HIGH pressure for 12 minutes. Allow for a 5-minute Natural Pressure Release, followed by a quick release for the rest.

5) Open lid and remove pork chops from the pot. Give rice mixture a good stir. Serve rice topped with your pork chops. ENJOY!!

**PRO TIP: For extra creamy pork chops, heat up another can of cream of mushroom soup to serve on top!

Pure Pressure Stuffed-Crust Pizza

Ingredients

- 1 can refrigerated pizza dough
- ½ cup favorite pizza sauce
- 1 cup mozzarella cheese, shredded
- 2 mozzarella cheese sticks (or any mozzarella cheese will work)
- Favorite toppings (I used mini pepperoni, green pepper, mushrooms)
- Non-stick cooking spray
- Aluminum foil

To Prepare:

1) Generously spray spring form (or any) pan with non-stick cooking spray. Spread pizza dough along the bottom of the pan.

2) Near the outer edge of where the crust would be, slice and line your cheese sticks in a complete circle around the pizza. Roll edge of dough over the cheese to completely cover it, then spread your dough back out.

3) Add ½ cup of pizza sauce to the middle and spread evenly. Cover with your favorite toppings. Cover spring form pan with aluminum foil.

4) Add 2 cups water to your pressure pot and lower the spring form pan in with a foil sling. Close lid and seal. Cook on manual HIGH pressure for 17 minutes. Quick release the pressure.

5) THIS STEP IS OPTIONAL. Remove pizza from spring form pan and place onto baking pan. Put in the oven to BROIL until desired crispiness. (At this stage I also add more mozzarella to the top of pizza and top my crust with butter/cheese) ENJOY!!

Savory Shrimp Scampi

Ingredients

• 8oz of your favorite thin pasta (I used veggie noodles for a healthier version)

• 2 cups chicken broth

• 2 Tbsp butter

• 2 Tbsp parsley

• 1 tsp salt

• 1 tsp pepper

• 2 cloves garlic, minced

• ½ freshly squeezed lemon

• 2 cups frozen cooked shrimp (I used tail-off, but tail-on adds more flavor)

To Prepare:

1) First, add your 2 cups chicken broth, followed by the remaining ingredients. (Make sure to break your noodles in half if needed)

2) Close lid & seal your pot. Set to cook on manual HIGH pressure for 5 minutes. Allow for a 5 min Normal Pressure Release and Quick Release any remaining steam.

3) Give it a good stir. SERVE & ENJOY!!

PRO TIP: After cooking, add 1 cup baby spinach, ½ cup heavy cream and ½ cup parmesan cheese, and use your sauté mode until it thickens for a "Creamy Shrimp Scampi"

Gratifying Gwumpkies (Cabbage Rolls)

Ingredients

- 1 cup brown or long grain white rice
- 1 large head cabbage
- 1 large egg
- 1 cup chopped onion
- 4 cloves garlic, minced
- 1 1/2 tsp salt
- 1/2 tsp freshly ground black pepper
- 2 lbs. ground beef
- 1 Tbsp oil

SAUCE

- 2 Tbsp butter
- 1 cup finely chopped onion
- 3 cloves garlic, minced
- 2 (14 1/2 oz. each) cans diced tomatoes (with juice)
- 1 (8 oz.) can tomato sauce
- 1/4 cup white vinegar
- 2 tsp low sodium instant beef bouillon
- 1/2 tsp garlic powder
- 1 tsp onion powder
- 1/2 tsp black pepper or freshly ground black pepper
- 3-4 dashes Worcestershire sauce
- 1 Tbsp cornstarch
- 2 Tbsp water
- Chopped fresh parsley for garnish

To Prepare:

1) Place 2 cups water in pressure pot along with head of cabbage. Cook on manual HIGH pressure for 10 minutes. Quick Release the pressure.

2) Open lid and remove cabbage. Empty remaining water. Press sauté mode.

3) Begin peeling your cabbage (try to leave yourself good size pieces for rolls).

4) While peeling cabbage, add ground beef, 1 onion, garlic, salt & pepper into your pressure pot. Cook until beef is fully browned. Empty pot when done.

5) Now, add all the ingredients for the sauce into the bottom of your pressure pot.

6) Place trivet on top of sauce. Use additional cooking dish, add 1 cup rice, 1 cup water, and 1 Tbsp oil. Wrap cooking dish with aluminum foil and place on trivet. Close and seal lid. Cook on manual HIGH pressure for 8 minutes. Quick release steam.

7) Open lid and remove rice dish. Add rice into your ground beef mixture and give it a good stir.

8) Take 1-2 pieces of cabbage and place a good size scoop of the ground beef and rice mixture into the middle. Tuck each end in and roll the cabbage. (Use tooth pick to hold together if needed)

9) Remove some or all the sauce from the bottom of pressure pot. Then, place your cabbage rolls onto the trivet. (Wouldn't cook more than 7-8 at a time). Cover your cabbage rolls with the sauce that you had removed.

10) Close and seal lid. Cook on manual HIGH pressure for 8 minutes. Quick release steam. Serve & ENJOY!!

Country-Style Steak and Mashed Potatoes

Ingredients

- 1-2lbs of your favorite steak (I used a thinner-cut top sirloin, but thick- cut cook just as well)
- 1 10 oz can French onion soup
- 1 packet of Au Jus Gravy Mix
- 2 tsp salt
- 2 tsp pepper
- 2 Tbsp corn starch
- 3-4 potatoes, cubed
- 4 cloves garlic, minced
- 4 Tbsp butter
- Aluminum foil

To Prepare:

1) Add 1 cup water, 10oz can of French onion soup, and your steaks to the pressure pot.

2) Sprinkle Au Jus gravy mix evenly over steaks, along with 1 tsp salt & pepper. Then, place trivet on top of steaks,

3) Place your potatoes in a separate cooking dish. Top with 4 Tbsp butter, 4 cloves garlic, 1 tsp salt & pepper. Cover with aluminum foil and place on trivet.

4) Close and seal lid. Cook on manual HIGH pressure for 15 minutes. Allow for a 5-minute Normal Pressure Release, followed by a Quick Release.

5) Open lid and remove potatoes. Use a hand mixer to mash your potatoes.

6) Remove steaks from bottom of pan. Turn pressure cooker to sauté mode and add 2 Tbsp corn starch. Whisk until fully dissolved. Serve gravy over mashed potatoes and steaks. ENJOY!

Loaded Chicken Ranch Potato Bake

- 1 Tbsp parsley to garnish
- 1 tsp salt
- 1 tsp pepper
- ½ Tbsp garlic powder

Ingredients

- 2 large boneless chicken breasts
- 3 slices of cooked bacon, chopped
- 6 red potatoes, cubed
- 1/2 cup chicken broth
- 1/2 cup milk
- 1/2 cup plain Greek yogurt
- 1 Tbsp butter
- 1 tsp olive oil
- 1 cup shred cheddar cheese
- 1/2 cup shredded mozzarella cheese
- 2 green onions, chopped
- 1 tsp chives
- 1 packet of Hidden Valley Ranch Dressing mix
- 1 tsp paprika

To Prepare:

1) Press sauté mode to heat pressure pot. Add olive oil, chicken breasts, garlic powder, salt & pepper to the pressure pot and cook until breasts are lightly browned on each side.

2) Add potatoes and ½ cup chicken broth to your pressure pot. Make sure to deglaze your pot if needed.

3) Close and seal lid. Cook on manual HIGH pressure for 10 minutes. Allow for a 10-minute Natural Pressure Release, then quick release any remaining steam.

4) Open lid and remove chicken breasts to shred. Also, make sure to mash your potatoes inside the

pot with a hand masher or mixer.

5) Add chicken back to the pot, along with any remaining ingredients (save ½ cup of shredded cheddar cheese). Give it a good stir.

6) Spray a casserole or cooking dish with non-stick cooking spray and transfer your ingredients.

7) Top with cheese and broil until cheese is melted. Serve and ENJOY!

Pure Pressure Corned Beef & Cabbage Dinner

Ingredients

- 5 cloves of garlic
- 2.5-3 lb. corned beef brisket, including its spice packet
- 2 lbs. of gold potatoes, quartered
- 3 cups baby carrots
- 1 head green cabbage, cut into wedges

To Prepare:

1) Add 4 cups water and trivet to your pressure pot. Then, add corned beef brisket along with its spice packet sprinkled on top.

2) Close and seal lid. Cook on manual HIGH pressure for 90 minutes. Allow for a 10-minute Natural Pressure Release, then Quick Release any remaining steam.

3) Open lid and remove brisket and trivet. Cover it with aluminum foil while veggies cook.

4) Now, add your potatoes, cabbage, and carrots to the pressure pot, along with the remaining juices from the brisket.

5) Cook on manual HIGH pressure for 5 minutes. Quick release the steam.

6) Uncover brisket and slice to desired portion. Serve with cabbage, potatoes, carrots and ENJOY!

Jammin' Jambalaya

- 1 (14.5 oz.) can of diced tomatoes
- Sliced scallions (optional)

Ingredients

- 1 tsp olive oil
- 8 oz Andouille sausage, sliced
- 2 boneless chicken breasts
- 1 1/4 cups uncooked long-grain brown rice
- 1 onion, chopped
- 1 red pepper, chopped
- 1 green pepper, chopped
- 2 stalks celery, chopped
- 1 tsp thyme
- 1/4 tsp ground red pepper
- 3 bay leaves
- 2 tsp Old Bay seasoning
- 1 tsp salt
- 1 tsp pepper
- 3 cloves garlic, minced
- 1lb cooked jumbo shrimp (I use tail-less for this)

To Prepare:

1) Press sauté mode on your pressure pot. Once hot, add 1 tsp olive oil, garlic, salt, pepper, Andouille sausage and chicken breasts and cook until they are lightly browned.

2) Add 2 ½ cups of water to your pressure pot. Make sure to deglaze pot if necessary. Now, add all the ingredients except for the shrimp and diced tomatoes.

3) Close and seal lid. Cook on manual HIGH pressure for 18 minutes. Quick release the steam.

4) Open lid and add the shrimp and diced tomatoes. Press sauté mode and cook for 4-5 minutes until shrimp are fully warmed. Serve & Enjoy!!

Pure Pressure Mongolian Beef

Ingredients

- 1lb. flank steak, sliced across the grain
- 1 Tbsp cornstarch
- 1 Tbsp olive oil
- 2/3 cup brown sugar
- 10 cloves of garlic, minced
- 1 Tbsp ginger, minced
- 1/2 cup soy sauce
- 1 tsp crushed red pepper flakes
- 2 Tbsp corn starch
- ¼ cup green onions
- 1 tsp sesame seeds
- 1 cup white rice
- 1 Tbsp butter
- Aluminum foil

To Prepare:

1) Add sliced beef to a large zip-lock bag, add 1 Tbsp cornstarch and shake well to coat the beef evenly.

2) Press sauté on your pressure pot. When hot, add oil and beef and cook for 2-3 minutes until beef is nice and warm.

3) Add the rest of the ingredients to the pot, except for corn starch, green onions, and sesame seeds. Give it a good stir so everything is covered in sauce.

4) Place trivet on top of beef mixture. In a cooking dish, add 1 cup rice, 1 cup water, and 1 Tbsp butter. Cover with aluminum foil and place on trivet.

5) Close lid and pressure cook on manual HIGH pressure for 8 minutes. Allow for a 10-minute Normal Pressure Release and

Quick Release any remaining steam.

6) Open lid and remove rice and trivet.

7) In a mixing bowl, add 2 Tbsp corn starch and ½ cup water. Whisk until slurry. Pour mixture into pressure pot.

8) Use sauté mode to cook for additional 2-3 minutes.

9) Serve over rice and garnish with fresh chopped green onions and sesame seeds. ENJOY!!

Irresistible Fall Off the Bone Ribs

Ingredients

• 3-4 lbs. baby back ribs (Cut big racks into smaller ones)

• 1 Tbsp salt

• 1 Tbsp pepper

• 1 Tbsp garlic salt

• 4 1/2 cups apple juice

• ½ cup apple cider vinegar

• Favorite BBQ Sauce (I use Sweet Baby Ray's Honey BBQ)

To Prepare:

1) First, remove the membrane from your rack of ribs. (This can easily be done by gripping it with a paper towel and pulling down) Then, season your ribs with garlic salt, salt & pepper.

2) Add 4 ½ cups apple juice and ½ cup apple cider vinegar to your pressure pot. Place trivet in bottom of pot and carefully stack ribs upright.

3) Close and seal lid. Cook on manual HIGH pressure for 30 minutes. Allow for a 5-minute Natural Pressure Release and Quick release any remaining steam.

4) Open lid and remove ribs. Smother top AND bottom of rack with your favorite BBQ sauce.

5) Place on baking sheet and BROIL in your oven until BBQ sauce starts to caramelize. Serve with your favorite Pure Pressure sides and ENJOY!!

Pure Pressure Breaded Boneless Chicken

Ingredients

• 3-4 Boneless chicken breasts (unfrozen)

• 1 pack of Kraft Shake'N Bake seasoning

• 1 tsp salt

• 1 tsp pepper

To Prepare:

1) Put Shake'N Bake seasoning in a zip-lock bag along with salt, pepper, and chicken breasts. Shake chicken breasts until completely seasoned.

2) Add 2 cups water and steam basket (see back of book). Place chicken breasts in basket.

3) Close and seal lid. Cook on manual HIGH pressure for 8 minutes. Allow for a 5-minute Natural Pressure Release and Quick Release any remaining steam.

4) Open lid and remove basket. Serve chicken with your favorite Pure Pressure recipe and ENJOY!

**PRO TIP: This chicken goes great in our Pure Pressure Chicken Parm. Recipe!

Creamy Buffalo Chicken Mac

Ingredients

• 2 boneless chicken breasts (unfrozen)

• ½ cup Frank's Red-Hot Sauce (plus a little extra to smother chicken breasts)

• 1lb. of your favorite macaroni pasta (I prefer Cavatappi for this!)

• 5 Tbsp butter

• 1 tsp salt

• 1 tsp pepper

• 1 tsp ground mustard

• 1 can evaporated milk (5oz)

• 6 cups Velveeta cheese, shredded or cut into small cubes (6 cups are 3/4ths of the standard 32. oz block of Velveeta)

To Prepare:

1) Press sauté mode on your pressure pot. When hot, add 1 Tbsp butter, boneless chicken breasts, salt & pepper. Cook for 4-5 minutes until nicely browned.

2) Remove chicken breasts from the pressure pot and smother each of them with Frank's Red-Hot Sauce.

3) Add 4 cups water to pressure pot and deglaze from cooking chicken. Then, add pasta, 4 Tbsp butter, and 1 tsp ground mustard to the pot.

4) Place steam basket (or elevated trivet) in pressure pot on top of pasta. Place chicken breasts in basket.

5) Close and seal lid. Cook on manual HIGH pressure for 5 minutes. Allow for a 5-minute Natural Pressure Release and Quick Release any remaining steam.

6) Open lid, remove steam basket and chicken breasts.

Then, press sauté mode on your pressure cooker.

7) Add 1 can evaporated milk and 6 cups Velveeta cheese to the pasta and stir continuously until cheese is nice and melted.

8) Once cheese is melted, stir in ½ cup Frank's Red-Hot Sauce.

9) Serve pasta topped with your chicken breasts and ENJOY!!

Ingredients

- 1 spaghetti squash
- 1 lb. ground turkey burger
- 1 Tbsp extra virgin olive oil
- 1 tsp salt
- 1 tsp pepper
- ½ Tbsp Oregano
- 1 jar of your favorite spaghetti sauce (I use Bertolli for this)
- 1 green pepper, diced
- 1 onion, diced
- 1 (14.5oz.) can of diced tomatoes

Stunning Spaghetti Squash

To Prepare:

1) Add 1 cup of water and spaghetti squash to pressure pot. Close and seal lid.

2) Cook on manual HIGH pressure for 10 minutes, then Quick Release the steam.

3) Open lid and remove spaghetti squash. Cut it in half lengthwise or else you won't get the right texture for spaghetti. Then, remove seeds and use a fork to string your spaghetti.

4) Empty any remaining water from pressure pot. Press sauté mode to heat.

5) Once pressure cooker is hot, add 1 Tbsp oil and turkey burger. Cook until burger is lightly browned. Then, add green pepper and onion and continue to cook until burger is done.

6) Add Oregano, spaghetti sauce, and diced tomatoes to the pot and continue to stir until sauce is fully warmed.

7) Serve meat and sauce mixture over your spaghetti squash and ENJOY!!

Pure Pressure Chicken Parm'

Ingredients

- 2-3 boneless chicken breasts
- 1 Tbsp butter
- 1lb of your favorite pasta (I use Cavatappi again in this recipe)
- 1 (14.5oz.) can of diced tomatoes
- 1 jar of your favorite spaghetti sauce
- 1 cup shredded parmesan cheese
- 1 Tbsp Oregano
- 1 tsp salt
- 1 tsp pepper

To Prepare:

1) Press sauté mode on your pressure cooker. When hot, add 1 Tbsp butter, chicken breasts, salt & pepper. Cook for 5 minutes until chicken is nice and browned.

2) Remove chicken breasts from the pressure pot. Add ½ cup of water and deglaze your pot.

3) Add pasta to the pressure pot. Fill with enough water to barely cover the top of your pasta.

4) Add steam basket (or elevated trivet) on top of your pasta. Add chicken breasts to the basket.

5) Close and seal lid. Cook on manual HIGH pressure for 5 minutes. Allow for a 5-minute Natural Pressure Release and then Quick Release the remaining steam.

6) Open lid and remove steam basket and chicken breasts. Now, add diced tomatoes, spaghetti sauce, & Oregano to

the pot. Use sauté mode and cook until sauce is fully warmed.

7) Serve chicken on pasta, topped with parmesan cheese and extra spaghetti sauce. Add yummy and crusty bread, ENJOY!!

Pure Pressure Healthy Stuffed Chicken

Ingredients

• 2-3 boneless chicken breasts

• ¼ cup low-fat shredded mozzarella cheese

• 2 (14.5oz.) cans of chopped artichoke hearts

• 1 Tbsp tsp sundried tomatoes, chopped

• 5 large basil leaves

• 1 clove of garlic

• ½ tsp curry

• ½ tsp paprika

• 1 tsp pepper

• Toothpicks

To Prepare:

1) Cut chicken breasts about halfway through with a sharp knife.

2) In a mixing bowl, mix and chop up mozzarella, basil, sundried tomatoes, garlic, and artichoke hearts.

3) Stuff your chicken breasts chunks with the artichoke mixture and stab with a toothpick to hold them together.

4) Add 1 cup of water steam basket (or trivet) to your pressure pot. Place chicken breasts in the basket.

5) Cook on manual HIGH pressure for 11 minutes. Allow for a 5-minute Natural Pressure Release and Quick Release any remaining pressure.

6) Open lid, remove chicken and toothpicks. Serve with your favorite veggie or side and ENJOY!

Out of This "WOODS", Venison Tips & Gravy

Ingredients

• 2lbs of venison tips (or sirloin will do)

• 2 Tbsp olive oil

• 1 onion, diced

• 2 cups beef broth

• 1/2 cup Flour

• 1 small can of mushrooms (optional)

• 1 Tbsp A1 steak sauce

• 1 tsp salt

• 1 tsp pepper

• 1 cup white rice

• 1 Tbsp butter

• Aluminum foil

To Prepare:

1) Press sauté mode to heat your pressure cooker. When hot, add 2 Tbsp oil, salt, pepper, and your venison tips.

2) Continue cooking until they start to lightly brown. Then, add your diced onion and mushrooms.

3) Once venison has fully browned, add 2 cups beef broth and make sure to deglaze your pot if necessary.

4) Place trivet over your steak tips for cooking the rice.

5) In a cooking dish, combine 1 cup white rice, 1 Tbsp butter, and 1 cup water. Cover it with aluminum foil and place on trivet.

6) Close and seal lid. Cook on manual HIGH pressure for 10 minutes. Allow for a 5-minute Natural Pressure Release and Quick Release any remaining pressure.

7) Open lid and remove rice and trivet.

8) In a cup or bowl, dissolve ½ cup flour and 1 ½ cups water until they make a nice slurry. Now add this slurry to your venison tips and stir continuously until you have a nice thick gravy.

9) Fluff your rice with a fork and serve topped with venison tips and gravy. ENJOY!

Gotta Get More, Goulash

Ingredients

- 2 tsp olive oil
- 1 lb. ground beef
- 1 large onion, diced
- 1 cup celery, diced
- 2 bay leaves
- 1 1/2 tsp Italian seasoning
- 1/2 tsp pepper
- ½ tsp salt
- 1 tsp Salt
- 4 cloves of garlic, minced
- 1 1/2 Tbsp Worcestershire Sauce
- 1 green pepper, chopped
- 4 cups chicken broth
- 2 cups favorite pasta (Cavatappi… you know by now)
- 1 Tbsp paprika
- 1 (14.5oz) can of diced tomatoes (with juices)
- 1 (14.5oz) can tomato sauce
- 2 cups cheese
- ¼ cup parsley, to garnish

To Prepare:

1) Press sauté mode to heat your pressure pot. When hot, add oil, ground beef, onion, celery, green pepper, bay leaves, salt & pepper. Cook until beef is browned.

2) Once browned, add Italian seasoning, Worcestershire sauce, and garlic. Continue to sauté for a couple of minutes.

3) Add broth and deglaze your pot if necessary. Then, add pasta and paprika. Give everything a good stir.

4) Now add your diced tomatoes and tomato sauce.

5) Close and seal your lid. Cook on manual HIGH pressure for 5 minutes. Allow for a 5-minute

Natural Pressure Release and Quick Release any remaining steam.

6) Open lid and stir in cheese & parsley. Serve with yummy bread and ENJOY!

Pure Pressure Pulled Pork/ Chicken

Ingredients

• 3-4lb boneless pork loin (or boneless chicken breasts)

• 1 onion, diced

• 1 tsp salt

• 1 tsp pepper

• 1 tsp paprika

• 1/2 Tbsp garlic salt

• 1 tsp liquid smoke

• 1 (14.5oz) can chicken broth

• ¼ cup chopped parsley (optional)

• 1 bottle of favorite BBQ sauce (Again, I use Sweet Baby Ray's Honey BBQ)

To Prepare:

1) Season meat with salt, pepper, paprika, & garlic salt.

2) Add 1 can chicken broth, 1 tsp liquid smoke, and trivet to the pressure pot. Set meat on the trivet.

3) Close and seal lid.

***For PORK, cook on manual HIGH pressure for 60 minutes. Allow a 10-minute Natural Pressure Release and then Quick Release any remaining steam.

***For CHICKEN, cook on manual HIGH pressure for 15 minutes. Allow for a 5-minute Natural Pressure Release and Quick Release any remaining steam.

4) Open lid and drain all but about ¼ cup of the liquid. Now shred your meat with a fork (or hand-mixer) and stir in favorite BBQ sauce.

5) Serve on a warm Kaiser bun with your favorite toppings! ENJOY!

Pure Pressure Chicken Tikka-Masala

Ingredients

• 1 ½ lb. boneless chicken (dark meat is best with this recipe)

• 2 Tbsp butter

• 1 cup white rice

• 1 cup Tikka-Masala sauce

• 1 onion, diced

• 1 cup frozen carrots (I used frozen here)

• 1 cup broccoli (Again, I used frozen.)

• 1 tsp salt

• 1 tsp pepper

• 1 Tbsp garlic powder

• 1 cup chicken broth

• 1 Tbsp parsley to garnish

To Prepare:

1) Press sauté mode on your pressure cooker. When hot, add 1 Tbsp butter, chicken, salt & pepper to the pot. Cook for about 5 minutes until chicken is a nice brown color.

2) Add 1 cup chicken broth and deglaze your pot if necessary. Then, add the remaining ingredients to the pot.

3) Close and seal lid. Cook on manual HIGH pressure for 5 minutes. Allow for a 5-minute Natural Pressure Release and then Quick Release the remaining steam.

4) Open lid and remove chicken to shred. (this part is optional, it's great either way!) Then, place it back in the pot and give it a good stir.

5) Garnish with parsley. Serve & ENJOY!

Pure Pressure Meatloaf & Taters

Ingredients

Potatoes

- 1.5 lbs. of Gold Little Potatoes
- 1 cup chicken broth (water works fine too)
- 1 clove of garlic, minced
- 4 Tbsp butter
- 1/2 cup shredded Parmesan cheese
- dried parsley (optional)
- Non-stick cooking spray

Meatloaf

- 1.5 lbs. ground beef
- 3/4 cup milk
- 1 egg
- 2 cups crushed saltine crackers
- 1 Tbsp Worcestershire sauce
- ½ Tbsp onion powder
- 1 tsp salt
- 1 tsp dry ground mustard
- 1 tsp pepper
- 1/2 Tbsp garlic powder
- 1 (14.5oz) can of diced tomatoes
- 1 green pepper, diced
- 1 onion, diced
- Aluminum foil

Meatloaf Glaze

- 1 cup ketchup
- 1 Tbsp brown sugar

To Prepare:

1) Spray pressure pot with non-stick cooking spray, then add little gold potatoes.

2) Add the remaining ingredients for the potatoes. Then, place the trivet on top of the potatoes.

3) In a mixing bowl, combine all the ingredients for the meatloaf and mash with your hands for a couple of minutes until everything looks blended in well.

Form into a rectangular shape like meatloaf.

4) Next, rip a big piece of aluminum foil and fold it into a nice boat-shaped dish for your meatloaf. Spray aluminum foil with non-stick spray and then place meatloaf in the boat.

5) Whisk ketchup and brown sugar together in a cup or bowl to create the glaze. Then, spread half of the glaze on the meatloaf and save the rest for later.

6) Place meatloaf boat on the trivet. Close and seal lid. Cook on manual HIGH pressure for 30 minutes, Quick Releasing the pressure.

7) Open lid and remove meatloaf boat. Smother the rest of the glaze on top of the meatloaf.

8) Lastly, add boat to a baking sheet and place in the oven on BROIL for 2-3 minutes until sauce caramelizes. Serve with your little potatoes and ENJOY!

Fiesta Chicken Taco Bowls

Ingredients

- 1 1/2 cups chicken broth
- 2 boneless chicken breasts
- 1 packet taco seasoning
- 1 (15oz.) can of black beans, drained and rinsed.
- 1 cup corn
- 1 1/2 cups salsa
- 1 1/4 cups long grain white rice, drained and rinsed.
- Non-stick cooking spray

Optional Toppings

- cheese
- chopped cilantro
- sliced avocado
- chopped green onion
- sour cream

To Prepare:

1) Spray bottom of pressure pot with non-stick cooking spray.

Then add ½ cup chicken broth and boneless chicken breasts.

2) Sprinkle chicken with taco seasoning.

3) Add black beans, corn, salsa, rice, and remaining 1 cup chicken broth to the pot. Give it a good stir to make sure rice is fully submerged into broth.

4) Close and seal lid. Cook on manual HIGH pressure for 8 minutes. Allow for a 12-minute Natural Pressure Release and then Quick Release any remaining steam.

5) Fluff rice with a fork. Then put lid back on and allow to sit for 5 minutes or so while you prep the toppings.

6) Once toppings are ready, remove and shred chicken breasts, then add back to the pot.

7) Lastly, add a scoop of taco mixture to a bowl. Top with some shredded chicken, and other favorite toppings. Serve with tortillas and ENJOY!!

Pure Pressure Stuffed Peppers

Ingredients

• 6 green peppers (or whatever your favorite color is!)

• 1 cup cooked white rice

• 1 lb. ground beef

• 1 egg, beaten

• 2 tsp garlic powder

• 1 1/2 tsp onion powder

• 1 tsp salt

• 1/2 tsp pepper

• 1/2 tsp thyme

• 1/2 tsp oregano

• 1 Tbsp paprika

• 1 Tbsp Worcestershire sauce

• 1/2 cup ketchup

• 1 (15oz.) can tomato sauce

• 3/4 cup Shredded Cheese, optional

To Prepare:

1) Cut the tops off your peppers, then remove the seeds and membrane. After that, poke 2-3 small holes in the bottom of your peppers to allow the liquid to drain.

2) In a mixing bowl, add all the ingredients except for the ketchup and tomato sauce. Mash until everything is fully blended (like a meatloaf).

3) In a separate bowl, mix ketchup and tomato sauce. Add half of this sauce to your meat mixture and mix it well.

4) Evenly disperse meat mixture into your peppers. Fill each pepper just shy of the top. Then, evenly spread the remaining sauce on top of peppers.

5) Add 1 cup water and trivet to bottom of pressure pot. Place peppers on trivet.

6) Close lid and seal. Cook on manual HIGH pressure for 17 minutes. Allow for a 7-minute Natural Pressure Release and

then Quick Release any remaining steam.

7) Open lid and remove peppers. Use a meat-thermometer to make sure ground beef is fully cooked. Should reach internal temp of 160 degrees. If needed, cook in additional 5-minute increments until you reach the minimum temp.

8) You can top peppers with optional shredded cheese, or hot sauce to give a little kick! ENJOY!!

Full-Flavored Cheeseburger & Tater' Slices

over both sides of all burger patties.

2) Add 1 cup chicken broth (or water) and potatoes to your pressure pot. Then place the trivet on top of the potatoes.

3) Make aluminum foil bowls for your burgers. Place foil bowls along with the burgers on the trivet.

4) Close and seal lid. Cook on manual HIGH pressure for 12 minutes. Allow for a 5-minute Natural Pressure Release and Quick Release any remaining steam.

5) Open lid and remove burgers from foil bowls. Place them on a baking sheet and top with slice of cheese.

6) Now scoop your potatoes from the pot and onto the baking sheet, as well. Top the potatoes with shredded cheddar cheese and optional bacon bits.

7) Place baking sheet in oven on BROIL until cheese is fully melted. Put burgers on bun with your favorite toppings and serve with cheesy potatoes. ENJOY

Ingredients

- 1-2 lbs. ground beef
- 1 Tbsp salt
- 1 Tbsp pepper
- ½ Tbsp garlic powder
- Favorite sliced cheese
- Favorite burger buns
- Favorite burger toppings
- 3-4 medium Russet potatoes, sliced
- 1 cup chicken broth (or water)
- 1 cup shredded cheddar cheese
- Bacon bits for topping (optional)
- Aluminum foil

To Prepare:

1) Separate ground beef into ½ lb. patties. Mix seasonings together and sprinkle evenly

APPETIZERS

Pure Pressure Creamy Spin-Dip

- 1 tsp pepper
- 1 tsp onion powder

Ingredients

- 10oz frozen spinach, chopped
- 8oz cream cheese
- 16oz shredded parmesan cheese
- 8oz shredded mozzarella cheese
- ½ cup chicken broth
- 14oz can artichoke hearts, chopped
- ½ cup sour cream
- ½ cup mayo
- 3 cloves garlic (or 1 Tbsp garlic powder)
- 1 tsp salt

To Prepare:

1) Place everything in your pressure pot except for the parmesan & mozzarella cheeses. (Make sure to drain your Artichoke hearts first!!)

2) Close and seal lid. Cook on manual HIGH pressure for 4 minutes. Quick release the pressure.

3) Open lid and stir in parmesan & mozzarella cheese.

4) Transfer to a serving bowl, along with your favorite chips or pitas! ENJOY!

Red-Hot Buffalo Chicken Dip

Ingredients

- 2 boneless chicken breasts
- 2 (8oz) blocks of cream cheese
- 1 packet Hidden-Valley Ranch dressing mix
- 1 cup sour cream
- 2 Tbsp butter
- ¾ cup Frank's Red-Hot Buffalo Sauce
- 2 cups shredded mild- cheddar cheese
- Aluminum foil
- Favorite chips, crackers, pitas for serving

To Prepare:

1) Put the chicken, cream cheese, ranch seasoning, sour cream, butter, and hot sauce in the pressure pot.

2) Close and seal lid. Cook on manual HIGH pressure for 20 minutes. Allow for a 10-minute Natural Pressure Release, and Quick Release any remaining steam.

3) Take the chicken breasts out to shred. Place them back in the pot and mix well.

4) Add in the cheddar cheese and mix until fully melted. (Can use sauté mode if needed)

5) Serve with your favorite chips, crackers, or pita and ENJOY!!

"Guac-a-delic" Deviled Eggs

Ingredients

- 6 large eggs
- 2 ripe avocados
- 1 Tbsp lime juice
- 1/2 tsp salt
- 1 Tbsp sour cream
- 1 Tbsp chopped cilantro (plus extra to garnish)
- 1 serrano pepper (remove seeds to lessen heat)
- 1 Tbsp chopped green onion

To Prepare:

1) Place 1 cup of water in pressure pot, along with the trivet.

2) Set 6 large eggs on top of trivet. Close and seal lid. Cook on manual HIGH pressure for 5 minutes. Allow for a 5-minute Natural Pressure Release, and Quick Release any remaining steam. Then, place eggs in a bowl of cold ice-water for 5 more minutes.

3) Peel and slide your hard-boiled eggs, removing the yolks.

4) In a mixing bowl, add and mash your 2 avocados. Then add any remaining ingredients. Mix-well.

5) Add 2 egg yolks (4 halves) into your guacamole spread. Mash and mix-well.

6) Scoop guacamole into each egg-half. Top with additional cilantro. Serve & ENJOY!!

Homemade Honey BBQ Meatballs

Ingredients

- 1 egg, beaten
- 1/2 cup bread crumbs
- 1/2 onion, diced
- 1/4 cup parmesan cheese
- 1/2 tsp garlic powder
- 1/2 tsp salt
- 1/4 tsp pepper
- 1 tsp Worcestershire sauce
- 1 1/4 pounds ground beef
- 2 Tbsp butter
- Sweet Baby Ray's Honey BBQ (or your favorite sauce!)
- Toothpicks for serving

To Prepare:

1) In a mixing bowl, combine everything except for the 2 Tbsp butter. Mash with your hands until fully mixed. Then scoop meat into approximately 1-inch balls.

2) Press sauté mode on your pressure pot. When hot, add 2 Tbsp butter and meatballs to the pot. Continue to cook meatballs until browned on all sides.

3) Add BBQ sauce to the pot, deglaze if needed. Close and seal lid. Cook on manual HIGH pressure for 4 minutes and then Quick Release the steam.

4) Serve with toothpicks. ENJOY!

Pure Pressure Pizza Poppers

Ingredients

• 1 can of refrigerated pizza dough

• 2 cups shredded mozzarella cheese

• Mini Pepperonis (or any cooked meat)

• Green onion/parmesan/oregano (Optional)

• Favorite pizza sauce for dipping

• Non-stick cooking spray

• Aluminum foil

To Prepare:

1) Spray silicone egg-bite mold (see back of book) with non-stick cooking spray.

2) Roll dough into square and cut into approximately 1-inch strips. Roll into dough balls.

3) Push pepperonis and a pinch of mozzarella cheese into the middle of each dough ball. Make sure dough is completely covering your meat and cheese.

4) Place balls into egg-bite mold and cover with aluminum foil.

5) Add 2 cups water and trivet to pressure pot. Place egg-bite mold on trivet. Close and seal lid. Cook on manual HIGH pressure for 17 minutes and Quick Release the pressure.

6) Open lid and remove poppers from egg-bite molds. Place on baking sheet, top with extra mozzarella cheese, parmesan, oregano, and green onions. Place in oven on BROIL until cheese is melted on top.

7) Serve with your favorite pizza sauce. ENJOY!

Kickin' Buffalo Chicken Sliders

Ingredients

- 2 boneless chicken breasts
- 2 (8oz) blocks of cream cheese
- 1 packet Hidden-Valley Ranch dressing mix
- 1 cup sour cream
- 2 Tbsp butter
- ¾ cup Frank's Red-Hot Buffalo Sauce
- 2 cups shredded mild- cheddar cheese
- Slider buns (or Hawaiian Rolls)
- Lettuce
- Tomato
- Sliced provolone cheese
- Ranch dressing

To Prepare:

1) Put the chicken, cream cheese, ranch seasoning, sour cream, butter, and hot sauce in the pressure pot.

2) Close and seal lid. Cook on manual HIGH pressure for 20 minutes. Allow for a 10-minute Natural Pressure Release, and Quick Release any remaining steam.

3) Take the chicken breasts out to shred. Place them back in the pot and mix well.

4) Add in the cheddar cheese and mix until fully melted. (Can use sauté mode if needed)

5) Place ranch dressing, lettuce, tomato onto slider bun. Then scoop your chicken onto the bun and top with provolone cheese. ENJOY!

Delightful Deviled-Eggs

Ingredients

- 8 eggs
- 4 Tbsp mayo
- 2 tsp mustard
- 1 tsp salt
- 1 tsp pepper
- Paprika, to garnish

To Prepare:

1) Place 1 cup water and trivet into pressure pot. Place eggs onto trivet.

2) Close and seal lid. Cook on manual HIGH pressure for 5 minutes. Allow for a 5-minute Natural Pressure Release and Quick Release any remaining steam.

3) Open lid and remove eggs. Slice each egg in-half lengthwise and remove the yolks.

4) In a mixing bowl, add egg yolks, mayo, mustard, salt & pepper. Mash with a fork until it forms a smooth creamy texture.

5) Scoop yolk mixture back into each egg half. (Use a zip-lock bag to avoid a mess)

6) Top with paprika and ENJOY!

BREADS

Pure Pressure Banana Nut Bread

Ingredients

- ½ cup butter
- 1 cup sugar
- 2 large eggs
- 3 bananas, mashed
- 2 cups flour (make sure it is aerated or your bread will be rubber from too much flour)
- 1 ½ tsp baking soda
- ½ tsp salt
- 1 cup Walnuts
- 1 Tbsp pure vanilla extract
- Aluminum foil
- Non-stick cooking spray

To Prepare:

1) In a mixing bowl, mix together ½ cup butter, 2 large eggs, and 1 cup sugar until it is a nice creamy texture.

2) Slowly add mashed bananas, making sure to mix-well.

3) Now add all your dry ingredients, including Walnuts. Mix well.

4) Spray 6" Bundt pan with non-stick cooking spray. Pour batter evenly into pan and cover with aluminum foil.

5) Add 2 cups water to pressure pot and place trivet in bottom of pan. Set Bundt pan on trivet.

6) Cook on manual HIGH pressure for 55 minutes. Allow for a 10-minute Natural Pressure Release, then Quick Release any remaining steam.

7) Open lid and remove pan. Allow 5 minutes to cool down. Top with butter, serve, ENJOY!!

**Pro Tip: Add 1 cup of chocolate chips for a Chocolatey Banana Nut Bread!

Homemade Crusty Whole Wheat Bread

Ingredients

• 2 cups all-purpose flour

• 1 cup whole wheat flour

• 2 tsp Kosher salt (Do NOT use regular table salt)

• 1/2 tsp instant rise yeast

• 1 1/2 cups warm water

• Plastic wrap

• Parchment paper

To Prepare:

1) In a cooking bowl, whisk together both flours, salt, and yeast. Slowly add in water and continue mixing until dough starts to form. (Don't over mix it!)

2) Cover bowl with plastic wrap and place in your pressure pot. Your pressure cooker must have the "Yogurt" setting for this. Use your Yogurt mode to incubate dough for 3 and ½ hours.

3) When timer is done, empty dough from bowl onto a well-floured surface and roll around once or twice.

4) Place dough onto parchment paper in an oven-safe cooking pot with lid (Dutch-oven). Heat oven to 450 degrees and cook for 30 minutes.

5) Remove lid from cooking-pot and cook for an additional 10 minutes or until it is a beautiful golden brown. Serve warm with butter, ENJOY!!

Pure Pressure Cornbread

Ingredients

• 2 8.5oz packages of Jiffy Corn Muffin Mix

• 1 cup milk

• 2 large eggs

• Non-stick cooking spray

To Prepare:

1) In a mixing bowl, combine all the ingredients and mix until fully blended.

2) Spray 7" springform pan (Link to pan I used in the back of the book) with non-stick cooking spray. Pour batter into pan. Cover with aluminum foil and create a sling if your trivet does not have handles.

3) Pour 1 cup water into the pressure pot and place your trivet in the bottom. Place your springform pan on the trivet and close the lid. Cook on manual HIGH pressure for 20 minutes. Allow for a 10-minute Natural Pressure Release.

4) Uncover springform pan and allow it to cool for 5-10 minutes before releasing the spring. Serve hot with butter and ENJOY!!!

Pure Pressure "Monkey Bread"

Ingredients

DOUGH:

- 1 cup of milk, warmed
- Tbsp butter, melted
- 1/4 cup white sugar
- 2 1/4 tsp instant yeast
- 3 1/4 cups flour (plus extra to work with)
- 2 tsp salt

BROWN SUGAR COATING:

- 1 cup light brown sugar
- 2 tsp cinnamon
- 8 Tbsp butter, melted

GLAZE:

- 1 cup powdered sugar
- 2 Tbsp milk

MISC:

- Non-stick cooking spray
- Aluminum foil
- 6" Bundt Pan

To Prepare:

1) Spray Bundt pan with non-stick cooking spray.

2) **Dough:** In a mixing bowl, add 3 ¼ cups flour and 2 tsp salt, whisk together.

3) In another mixing bowl, add 1 cup warm milk, 1/3 cup warm water, ¼ cup sugar, 2 Tbsp melted butter, and 2 ¼ tsp instant yeast. Mix until yeast is dissolved.

4) Slowly add milk mixture to your flour mixture, making sure to mix it very well. (If your flour seems too wet, add 2 Tbsp flour at a time until desired consistency)

5) Spray empty mixing bowl with non-stick cooking spray, and transfer dough to this bowl. Cover with plastic wrap and allow 1-2 hours for dough to rise (or you can heat oven to 200 degrees, turn off, and allow dough to sit in heated oven to speed up the process)

6) Sugar coating: In a mixing bowl, mix together 1 cup brown sugar and 2 tsp cinnamon. Also, melt 8 Tbsp butter in a cup for dipping.

7) When dough is finished rising, form it into a nice 8-10" square. Cut dough into approximately 60 squares, and then roll each square into a ball.

8) Dip each dough ball into your melted butter, then roll in the brown sugar and cinnamon mixture.

9) Place each ball into your Bundt pan, making sure to stagger each seem that you create as you go. Cover Bundt pan with plastic wrap and again, allow to sit for at least 1 hour for dough to rise additional 1-2 inches in Bundt pan. (Oven can be used again to speed up the process)

10) Add 2 cups of water and trivet to your pressure pot. Remove plastic wrap from Bundt pan and replace with aluminum foil. Place Bundt pan on trivet.

11) Close lid and seal. Cook on manual HIGH pressure for 30 minutes, allowing for a 5-minute Natural Pressure Release. Quick release the remaining steam.

12) **Glaze:** Whisk together 1 cup powdered sugar and 2 Tbsp milk before bread is finished cooking.

13) Open lid and remove Bundt pan once timer beeps. Remove aluminum foil and pour glaze over hot Monkey bread. Allow 5-10 minutes to cool. Serve and ENJOY!!

Chocolate Banana Zucchini Bread

Ingredients

- 2 ripe bananas, mashed
- 1 zucchini, shredded
- 1 egg
- 1/2 cup vegetable oil
- 1 1/2 cups flour
- 1/2 tsp salt
- 1/3 cup white sugar
- 1/3 cup brown sugar
- 1/2 tsp baking powder
- 1 tsp baking soda
- 1 cup semi-sweet chocolate chips
- Non-stick cooking spray
- Aluminum foil

To Prepare:

1) Spray spring form pan (or preferably Bundt pan) with non-stick cooking spray.

2) In a mixing bowl, combine bananas, zucchini, egg, and oil. Whisk together.

3) In a separate bowl, whisk together flour, salt, sugars, baking powder and baking soda. Slowly add dry ingredients to the other mixing bowl, stirring continuously.

4) Once all of the ingredients are blended. Fold in chocolate chips. Move batter to your pan and cover with aluminum foil. Make sure to make a sling if using a spring form pan.

5) Add 2 cups water to your pressure pot and lower in the spring form pan.

6) Close and seal lid. Cook on manual HIGH pressure for 60 minutes and then Quick Release the pressure.

7) Open lid and remove bread. Serve with butter, (or my favorite, Peanut Butter) ENJOY!!

Soft N' Fluffy Homemade White Bread

Ingredients

- Non-stick cooking spray
- 2 cups flour
- ½ tsp baking soda
- 1 tsp salt
- 1¼ cup whole milk plain yogurt

To Prepare:

1) Spray a separate cooking bowl (big enough to hold 4-5 cups) with non-stick cooking spray.

2) In a mixing bowl, whisk together flour, baking soda, and salt. Once blended, use a fork to slowly mix in yogurt. Continue to stir until a nice dough has formed.

3) Roll your dough into a ball. (If you have trouble keeping it together sprinkle with warm water)

4) Add your dough to your cooking dish (NO LID) and cover with aluminum foil.

5) Add 4 cups water and trivet to pressure pot and then place your cooking dish on the trivet.

6) Close and seal lid. Cook on manual HIGH pressure for 25 minutes. Allow for a 10-minute Natural Pressure Release and Quick Release any remaining steam.

7) Open lid and remove bread. Serve warm with butter, ENJOY!

Pure Pressure Zucchini Bread

Ingredients

- 1-1/2 cups flour
- 1/2 tsp salt
- 1/2 tsp baking soda
- 1/2 tsp baking powder
- 1-1/2 tsp ground cinnamon
- 1 egg, plus 1 egg white
- 1/2 cup vegetable oil
- 1 cup sugar
- 1 tsp pure vanilla extract
- 1-1/2 cup grated zucchini (approx. 1 large or 2 smaller zucchini)
- ½ cup chopped walnuts (optional)
- Non-stick cooking spray
- Aluminum foil

To Prepare:

1) Spray 7" spring form pan (see back of book) with non-stick cooking spray, and also powder it with flour.

2) Sift flour, salt, baking powder, baking soda, and cinnamon together.

3) In a large bowl, beat eggs, oil, vanilla, and sugar.

4) Add sifted ingredients to the creamed mixture, and mix- well.

5) Stir in zucchini and nuts until well combined. Pour batter into prepared spring form pan. Cover pan with aluminum foil.

6) Add 1 cup water to pressure pot. Lower spring form pan with a foil sling into the pressure pot.

7) Close and seal lid. Cook on manual HIGH pressure for 60 minutes. Allow for a 10-minute Natural Pressure Release and Quick Release any remaining steam.

8) Open lid and remove aluminum foil from spring form pan. Dab bread with paper towel to absorb water if necessary.

9) Remove bread and serve warm with butter/cinnamon! ENJOY!

Soft as A Feather, Dinner Rolls

Ingredient

- 1 cup flour
- 1 tsp salt
- 1 tsp active dry yeast
- 2 Tbsp vegetable oil
- 1 Tbsp butter
- ½ Tbsp sugar
- Non-stick cooking spray
- Plastic wrap
- Aluminum foil
- 2 Tbsp Butter and 2Tbsp Milk (To Brush)

To Prepare:

1) In a mixing bowl, mix 6 Tbsp lukewarm water, ½ Tbsp sugar, and 1 tsp yeast. Allow this to sit until it starts to become a nice foamy texture.

2) Add 1 cup flour and ¼ tsp salt. Mix it up good with a spoon. Once dough starts to form, add 2 Tbsp oil and knead dough with your hands. (If necessary, you can add more flour to help knead dough)

3) Spray cooking bowl with non-stick cooking spray and then transfer your dough. Cover with plastic wrap.

4) Place in pressure cooker on "Yogurt" setting to incubate for 1 hour.

5) Once dough has risen, spray a 6" square baking dish with non-stick cooking spray.

6) Break dough evenly into 6-8 pieces and roll each of them into an individual ball. Transfer each ball to your baking dish. Cover with aluminum foil.

7) Add 2 cups water and trivet to pressure pot. Place baking dish on trivet.

8) Close and seal lid. Cook on manual HIGH pressure for 30 minutes. Quick Release the pressure.

9) Open lid, remove and uncover rolls. Whisk together your melted butter and milk and brush over top of rolls. Place in oven on BROIL until a nice golden-brown color. Serve warm with butter, or my favorite, CINNAMON BUTTER! ENJOY!!

DESSERTS

Marvelous Mini-Cheesecakes

10-15 seconds until it is broken up.

3) Stir in about half of the sugar mixture from above, mix-well. Then, add the remaining sugar and continue to stir until dissolved.

4) Slowly stir in ½ cup sour cream and 2tsp pure vanilla. Make sure not to over mix.

5) Stir in your eggs one at a time, until fully blended.

6) Pour cheesecake batter into mini pie crusts and then cover each pie with aluminum foil.

7) Add 2 cups water and trivet to pressure pot. Cook on manual HIGH pressure for 30 minutes. Allow for a 5-minute Normal Pressure Release, then Quick release any remaining steam.

8) Open lid and remove/uncover cheesecakes. Allow to cool down on stove for 15-20 minutes. Then, place cheesecakes in fridge to cool for an additional 4 hours to achieve the perfect texture.

9) Top with your favorite pie filling, serve, ENJOY!!!

Ingredients

• 16oz cream cheese, room temperature

• 2 large eggs, room temperature

• 2/3 cup white sugar

• 1/2 cup sour cream, room temperature

• 2 Tbsp cornstarch

• 2 tsp pure vanilla extract

• 1 tsp salt

• 1-2 packages of Keebler Ready Crust Mini Pies (batter is enough for 2)

• Aluminum foil

• Favorite pie toppings

To Prepare:

1) In a mixing bowl, mix 2 Tbsp cornstarch, 1 tsp salt, and 2/3 cup sugar.

2) In a separate mixing bowl, add cream cheese and stir for

Perfect Pineapple Upside-down Cake

Ingredients

- 1 cup pineapple juice
- 1/2 cup cooking oil
- 1 box of yellow cake mix
- 3 eggs
- Canned pineapple rings
- Maraschino cherries
- 1/2 cup brown sugar
- 1/4 cup butter
- Non-stick cooking spray
- Aluminum foil
- Favorite ice-cream (optional)

To Prepare:

1) In a mixing bowl, add yellow cake mix, ½ cup oil, 3 eggs, & 1 cup of pineapple juice. Mix until fully dissolved.

2) Line your ramekins (or spring-form pan) with non-stick cooking spray.

3) Add 1 Tbsp brown sugar and ½ Tbsp butter to each ramekin (or full amount of sugar/butter if using spring-form)

4) Next, place 1 pineapple ring in each ramekin (or several for big cake), followed with a cherry in the center of each.

Then, pour your batter over the top of the pineapples. Cover with aluminum foil.

5) Add 2 cups water to your pressure pot and place trivet in bottom of pan. Place cakes onto trivet and make sure you don't overload past the max fill.

6) Close and seal lid. Cook on manual HIGH pressure for 17 minutes. Quick release the pressure. Remove cake from the pot. Serve with your favorite ice-cream, ENJOY!

Pure Pressure Lemon Bars

Ingredients

- ¾ cups (1½ sticks) butter
- ½ cup sugar
- ¼ tsp salt
- 1 egg
- 2 cups flour
- 1 Tbsp lemon zest
- ½ tsp vanilla
- 1 jar (10-12 oz) of lemon curd
- Non-stick cooking spray
- Aluminum foil
- Powdered-sugar for topping (optional)

To Prepare:

1) In a mixing bowl, beat butter and sugar until fully mixed.

2) Add the salt, egg, lemon zest and vanilla; beat well.

3) Slowly add 1 cup of flour at a time until a soft-dough forms.

4) Spray 6" square baking pan (or spring-form) with non-stick cooking spray. Then, press dough evenly into the pan (or spring-form pan).

5) Spread lemon curd evenly on top of dough. Cover with aluminum foil.

6) Add 2 cups water to pressure pot and place trivet in the bottom of pan. Set your pan on top of trivet and close the lid.

7) Cook on manual HIGH pressure for 30 minutes. Quick release the pressure.

8) Open lid and remove pan. Allow 5 minutes to cool and then top with powdered-sugar (optional). SERVE AND ENJOY!

Chronic Carrot Cake

Ingredients

- 1 cup flour
- ½ tsp baking soda
- ¾ tsp baking powder
- ¼ tsp salt
- ½ tsp allspice
- ¼ tsp nutmeg
- 2 eggs
- ¼ cup of brown sugar
- 1/3 cup carrots, grated
- 1/3 cup sweetened flaked coconut
- 1/3 cup toasted pecans, chopped
- ½ cup sugar
- 4 Tbsp melted butter
- ¼ cup pineapple juice
- 3 Tbsp yogurt
- Jar of favorite cream cheese frosting (I make my own, mix together 1 8oz brick cream cheese, 1 stick of butter, 1 cup powdered sugar, and 1 tsp pure vanilla)

To Prepare:

1) In a mixing bowl, combine 1 cup flour, ½ tsp baking soda, ¾ tsp baking powder, ¼ salt, ½ tsp allspice, and ¼ tsp nutmeg.

2) In a second mixing bowl, combine 2 eggs, ¼ cup brown sugar, 1/3 cup carrots, 1/3 cup coconut, ½ cup sugar, 4 Tbsp melted butter, ¼ cup pineapple juice, and 3 Tbsp yogurt. Mix until fully blended.

3) Slowly mix ingredients together, just enough until the dry ingredients get wet.

4) Spray 7" springform pan (I posted a link of mine in the back) with non-stick cooking oil and pour in batter. Cover with aluminum foil and make a sling if your trivet does not have handles.

5) Add 2 cups water and place springform pan onto trivet.

Close and seal lid. Cook on manual HIGH pressure for 32 minutes. Allow for a 10-minute Normal Pressure Release and then Quick Release any remaining pressure.

6) Check your cake with a toothpick. If it is still moist, cook for another 5 minutes. If not, allow cake to cool before releasing spring. Top with your favorite cream cheese frosting and ENJOY!

Luscious Lava Cakes

Ingredients

- 2 eggs
- 4 Tbsp butter
- ¼ semi-sweet chocolate chips (plus a little extra for the centers)
- 4 Tbsp milk
- 1/3 cup flour
- ¼ tsp salt
- 1 Tbsp honey
- ½ tsp baking powder
- 1 Tbsp cocoa powder
- Non-stick cooking spray
- Aluminum foil
- Ice-cream/powdered sugar (optional)

To Prepare:

1) In a mixing bowl, add 4 Tbsp butter and ¼ cup chocolate chips. Place in microwave for about 30 seconds. (Might have to do it twice depending on how soft your butter is beforehand)

2) Add the remaining ingredients to the melted chocolate and whisk together until everything is fully dissolved.

3) Spray 3-4 ramekins with non-stick cooking spray. Fill each ramekin about ½ way with batter, then sprinkle in a few chocolate chips (more chips= more lava ☐). Top the chocolate chips with more batter and continue to fill ramekins until they are about ¾ full. Cover each ramekin with foil.

4) Add trivet or steam rack to your pressure pot, along with 1 ½ cups water. Add ramekins to the pot, then close and seal the lid. Cook on manual HIGH pressure for 4 minutes, or 5 minutes to thicken some of the lava. Quick release the pressure when timer is done.

5) Open lid and remove ramekins. Remove foil from each ramekin and cover with an individual plate for serving. Now give it a gentle flip to remove the cake from the ramekin. Add a scoop of your favorite ice-cream and/or top with powdered sugar!! ENJOY!

Death by Peanut-Butter Cheesecake

Ingredients

CRUST

- 1 cup crushed Oreo cookie crumbs
- 2 Tbsp butter melted

FILLING

- 12 oz. cream cheese, room-temp
- 1/2 cup sugar
- 1/2 cup peanut butter
- 1/4 cup heavy whipping cream
- 1 1/2 tsp pure vanilla extract
- 1 Tbsp flour
- 2 eggs, room temperature
- 1 egg yolk, room temperature
- 3/4 cup semisweet chocolate chips

TOPPING

- 6 oz. milk chocolate, shredded
- 1/3 cup heavy whipping cream
- 2/3 cup coarsely chopped Reese's peanut butter cups

MISC.

- Non-stick cooking spray
- Aluminum foil

To Prepare:

1) In a mixing bowl, combine 1 cup Oreo and 2 Tbsp melted butter, mix-well.

2) Spray a 7" spring form pan with non-stick cooking spray. Spread Oreo evenly across bottom of pan, then place in the freezer for at least 10 minutes.

3) In a mixing bowl, mix together cream cheese and ½ cup sugar until smooth. Then add in ½ cup peanut butter, ¼ cup heavy cream, 1 Tbsp flour, and 1 ½ tsp vanilla. Continue to stir.

4) Mix in eggs, one at a time, until fully blended. Then fold in chocolate chips.

5) Pour batter over your crust and cover spring form pan with

aluminum foil. Make sure to make a foil sling as well.

6) Add 2 cups water to the pressure pot and lower in the spring form pan. Close and seal lid. Cook on manual HIGH pressure for 55 minutes. Allow for a 10-minute Natural Pressure Release and then Quick Release any remaining steam.

7) Open lid, remove and uncover cheesecake. Let cool in refrigerator for at least 4 hours.

8) Once cheesecake is cooled, make your Ganache. Heat heavy cream on sauté mode until boiling, then add in shredded chocolate and whisk until it is a nice creamy chocolate.

9) Pour Ganache over your cheesecake and top with crushed Reese's peanut butter cups. ENJOY!!

White Chocolate Strawberry Cheesecake

Ingredients

CRUST

• 2 cups crushed Oreo cookie crumbs

• 4 Tbsp butter, melted

FILLING

• 2 (16oz) blocks of cream cheese, room-temp

• ½ cup sugar

• 1 cup strawberry jam

• ½ cup sour-cream

• 2 Tbsp flour

• 4 eggs, room-temp

TOPPINGS

• 6oz. white chocolate, finely chopped

• 1/3 cup heavy whipping cream

• Fresh strawberries

• Whipped Cream

MISC

• Non-stick cooking spray

• Aluminum foil

To Prepare:

1) In a mixing bowl, combine crushed Oreo and melted butter, mix-well.

2) Spray an 8" spring form pan with non-stick cooking spray. Spread Oreo evenly across bottom of pan, then place in the freezer for at least 10 minutes.

3) In a mixing bowl, mix cream cheese and sugar until nice and smooth. Slowly blend in jam, sour-cream, and flour. Then mix in your eggs one at a time until fully blended.

4) Pour batter over your crust and cover spring form pan with aluminum foil. Make sure to make a foil sling.

5) Add 2 cups water to pressure pot and lower spring form pan into pot.

6) Close and seal lid. Cook on manual HIGH pressure for 35 minutes. Allow for a 10-minute Natural Pressure Release and Quick Release any remaining steam.

7) Open lid, remove and uncover cheesecake. Let cool in refrigerator for at least 4 hours.

8) Once cheesecake is cooled, make your topping. Heat heavy cream on sauté mode until boiling, then add in white chocolate and whisk until it is a nice creamy texture.

9) Pour white chocolate over your cheesecake. Then top with fresh strawberries and whipped cream. ENJOY!

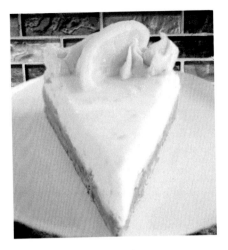

Lovely Lemon & Strawberry Cheesecake

Ingredients

CRUST

• 1 box Pillsbury Strawberry Cake Mix

• 1/2 cup unsalted butter, room-temp

• 1 Tbsp lemon juice

CHEESECAKE

• 16oz cream cheese, room-temp

• 3/4 cups sugar

• 1/2 cup sour cream

• 2 tsp pure vanilla extract

• 1/3 cup lemon juice

• zest of 2 lemons

• 2 eggs, room-temp

TOPPING

• 1/2 cup Pillsbury Strawberry Frosting

MISC

• Non-stick cooking spray

• Aluminum foil

To Prepare:

1) In a mixing bowl, combine cake mix, butter, and lemon juice. Mix until everything is fully blended.

2) Spray non-stick cooking spray into 7" spring form pan, then evenly press your crust into the pan. Place in freezer for at least 10 minutes.

3) In a mixing bowl, mix cream cheese and sugar until a nice creamy texture.

4) Mix in sour cream, vanilla, lemon juice, and lemon zest. Then, add in eggs one at a time and continue to stir until everything is fully blended. (Don't over stir)

5) Pour batter over crust and cover spring form pan with aluminum foil. Make sure to make a foil sling.

6) Add 2 cups water and lower spring form pan into pressure pot. Close and seal lid. Cook on manual HIGH pressure for 50

minutes. Allow for a 10-minute Natural Pressure Release and Quick Release any remaining steam.

7) Open lid, remove and uncover cheesecake. Allow to cool in refrigerator for at least 4 hours.

8) Once cooled, top with Strawberry frosting, lemon, and lemon zest. ENJOY!!

Pure Girl Scout Samoa Cheesecake

MISC

• Non-stick cooking spray

• Aluminum foil

Ingredients

CRUST

• 1 cup crushed chocolate graham crackers

• 2 Tbsp butter, melted

FILLING

• 12oz cream cheese, room-temp

• 1/2 cup sugar

• 1/4 cup heavy whipping cream

• 1/4 cup sour-cream

• 1/2 tsp pure vanilla extract

• 1 Tbsp flour

• 2 eggs, room-temp

• 1 egg yolk, room-temp

TOPPING

• 1 1/2 cups sweetened shredded coconut

• 12 chewy caramels

• 3 Tbsp heavy cream

• 1/4 cup chopped semisweet chocolate

To Prepare:

1) In a mixing bowl, whisk together crushed chocolate graham crackers and melted butter.

2) Spray 7" spring form pan with non-stick cooking spray and then press graham crackers evenly into the bottom of the pan. Place in the freezer for at least 10 minutes.

3) In a mixing bowl, mix together cream cheese and sugar until it has reached a creamy texture.

4) Blend in heavy cream, sour-cream, vanilla and flour. Then, mix in eggs one at a time until they are fully mixed.

5) Pour batter over crust and cover spring form pan with aluminum foil.

6) Add 2 cups water and trivet to pressure pot and place spring form pan on the trivet.

7) Close and seal lid. Cook on manual HIGH pressure for 30 minutes. Allow for a 10-minute Natural Pressure Release and Quick Release any remaining steam.

8) Open lid, remove and uncover cheesecake. Check with a toothpick to make sure it is done (If not, cook additional 5 minutes). If done, allow to refrigerate for additional 4 hours before topping.

9) Once cooled, start to prepare your toppings. Heat oven to 300 degrees and place coconut on baking sheet for 20 minutes, stirring every 5 minutes.

10) Place caramels and cream in a microwave-safe mixing bowl, and heat on HIGH for 1-2 minutes. Stir periodically until caramel is nice and smooth.

11) Add toasted coconut to caramel mixture and stir until blended. Pour evenly over your cheesecake.

12) Now place chocolate chips in the microwave for about 30 seconds, until melted. Once melted, transfer to a zip-lock bag and snip the corner. Drizzle chocolate beautifully across your cheesecake to make others drool. ENJOY!

Turtle-Egg Brownie Bites

Ingredient

• 1 box of your favorite brownie mix (I used Ghirardelli Double Chocolate)

• ¼ cup vegetable oil

• 1 egg

• ¼ cup water

• ½ cup crushed pecans (plus more for topping)

• 1 cup caramel, melted

• Non-stick cooking spray

• Aluminum foil

To Prepare:

1) Spray silicone egg-bite mold with non-stick cooking spray.

2) In a mixing bowl, combine brownie mix as instructed (Mix, Egg, Oil. Water).

3) Pour batter into egg-bite molds and cover with aluminum foil.

4) Add 1 cup water and trivet to your pressure pot. Place egg-bite mod on trivet.

5) Close and seal lid. Cook on manual HIGH pressure for 20 minutes. Allow for a 5-minute Natural Pressure Release and Quick Release any remaining steam.

6) Open lid, uncover and remove brownie bites from egg-bite mold. In a microwave-safe bowl, melt caramels for 30 seconds or until melted.

7) Pour melted caramel over brownie bites and top with extra crushed pecans. ENJOY!

Can't Stop BIRTHDAY POPS!

Ingredients

- 1 box of Pillsbury Funfetti Cake Mix
- 1/3 cup oil
- 1 cup water
- 3 eggs
- 2 cups white chocolate chips, melted
- 1 cup sprinkles
- Sucker sticks
- Non-stick cooking spray
- Aluminum foil

To Prepare:

1) In a mixing bowl, mix the cake mix according to the box (Mix, Oil, Water, Eggs).

2) Spray egg-bite mold with non-stick cooking spray. Then pour in batter about ¾ of the way full in each section. (Will cook more than 1 batch) Cover with aluminum foil.

3) Add 2 cups water and trivet to pressure pot. Place egg-bite mold on trivet.

4) Close and seal lid. Cook on manual HIGH pressure for 20 minutes. Allow for a 5-minute Natural Pressure Release and Quick Release any remaining steam,

5) Open lid, uncover and remove cake bites from mold. In a mixing bowl, melt white chocolate in microwave for 30 seconds or until melted.

6) Place sticks in each cake bite, dip and roll in melted white chocolate and top with sprinkles. ENJOY!!

**Pro Tip Make a stand out of Cardboard or Styrofoam before putting suckers together to make process a LOT easier!

Chocolate Peanut-Butter Swirl Cheesecake

Ingredients

CRUST

• 2 cups crushed Oreo cookies (about 24 cookies)

• 8 Tbsp butter, melted

FILLING

• 3 (11.5oz) container of cream cheese, room-temp

• 1 1/4 cups sugar

• 2 cups sour cream

• 1 cup heavy cream

• 4 large eggs, room-temp

• ½ cup bittersweet chocolate chips (I prefer Ghirardelli)

• ¾ cup peanut butter chips (Reese's, of course!)

• 1 tsp pure vanilla extract

MISC

• Non-stick cooking spray

• Aluminum foil

To Prepare:

1) Spray 8" spring form pan (7" is fine) with non-stick cooking spray.

2) In a mixing bowl, combine crushed Oreo cookies and melted butter. Mix- well and then press evenly into bottom of your spring form pan.

3) In a separate bowl, combine cream cheese and sugar and mix until it is a nice creamy texture.

4) Slowly mix in sour-cream. pure vanilla, and heavy cream. Then, mix in your eggs one at a time until blended. (Do not over mix!)

5) Put the chocolate and butterscotch chips in 2 separate small microwave-safe bowls. Microwave until melted, stirring every 30 seconds, about 1 minute 30 seconds.

6) Ladle 2 cups of cheesecake batter into a medium bowl and 2 cups into a second medium

bowl. Fold the melted butterscotch into one of the bowls until completely combined. Fold the melted chocolate into the other bowl until completely combined. Leave the remaining batter white.

7) Use an ice cream scoop or large spoon and drop scoopfuls of the batter onto the crust, alternating between the different flavors until all the batter is gone. Use a long wooden skewer and drag it through the batter, making sure the skewer reaches down to the bottom of the pan

to marble the colors for a tie-dye effect.

8) Cover spring form pan with aluminum foil. Make sure to make a foil sling.

9) Add 3 cups water and spring form pan to pressure pot. Close and seal lid. Cook on manual HIGH pressure for 60 minutes. Allow for a 10-minute Natural Pressure Release and Quick Release any remaining steam.

10) Open lid, uncover and remove cheesecake. Allow to refrigerate in spring form pan for at least 4 hours before serving. ENJOY!

Heavenly Angel Food Cake with Strawberry Topping

rise. Spoon the mixture into your 7" angel food cake pan and cover with aluminum foil.

5) Add 2 cups water and trivet to pressure pot. Place cake pan on trivet.

6) Close and seal lid. Cook on manual HIGH pressure for 27-minutes. Do the "Slow-Release" technique to remove your steam. (Slowly open lever)

7) Open lid, remove and uncover cake. Allow 5-10 minutes to cool. (If you can wait!)

8) Use a knife along the edge of the pan to help un-stick the cake.

9) Push the bottom of your cake up towards the center piece of the pan to remove.

10) Serve on a plate, topped with warm Strawberry Jam & ENJOY!!

**PRO TIP: Crush 1lb fresh strawberries, mixed with ½ cup sugar, for a quick homemade topping. Top with LOTS of whip cream!

Ingredients

- 1 box of Angel food cake mix (Betty Crocker)
- Strawberry Jam, warmed
- 5 oz water (for mix)
- Aluminum foil

To Prepare:

1) Use half of your angel food cake mix box which is 1.5 cups. Put into a bowl. (This makes 2 cakes!)

2) Combine cake mix with 5oz of water (1/2 cup +1/8 cup, you're welcome!)

3) Use a mixer to mix water and angel food cake mix for about a minute on high or until it starts to fluff up similar to meringue.

4) Do NOT grease your pan. The non-stick pan is enough, and it allows the cake to slowly

Unavoidable Cookies N' Cream Cheesecake

Ingredients

CRUST

• 1 cup crushed Oreos (12 cookies)

• 2 Tbsp butter, melted

CHEESECAKE

• 1 (16oz) block of cream cheese, room-temp

• 1/2 cup sugar

• 2 large eggs, room-temp

• 1Tbsp flour

• 1/4 cup heavy whipping cream

• 1 tsp pure vanilla extract

• 8 Oreo cookies, chopped

TOPPING

• 1 cup Cool Whip

• 8 whole Oreo cookies, coarsely chopped

• chocolate sauce (optional)

MISC

• Non-stick cooking spray

• Aluminum foil

To Prepare:

1) Spray 7" spring form pan with non-stick cooking spray.

2) In a small bowl, mix together 1 cup crushed Oreos and melted butter and then press into the bottom of your spring form pan. Freeze for at least 10-minutes.

3) In a mixing bowl, mix cream cheese and sugar until it is a nice and creamy texture.

4) Slowly add in the flour, heavy cream, and vanilla and mix until smooth. Then, add you eggs one at a time until they are fully incorporated

5) Now fold in your 8 chopped Oreo cookies and pour your batter onto your crust. Cover

pan with aluminum foil. Make sure to create a foil sling.

6) Pour 1 1/2 cups of water into the pressure pot and then lower in your cheesecake.

7) Close and seal lid. Cook on manual HIGH pressure for 35 minutes. Allow for a 10-minute Natural Pressure Release and Quick Release any remaining steam.

8) Open lid, remove and uncover cheesecake. Allow to refrigerate for at least 4 hours.

9) Once cooled, top with cool whip, chopped Oreos, and chocolate sauce! ENJOY!!

Marvelous Mint Chocolate Cheesecake

Ingredients

CRUST

• 2 cups crushed Oreo cookie crumbs

• 4 Tbsp butter, melted

FILLING

• 2 (16oz) blocks of cream cheese, room-temp

• ½ cup sugar

• 1 Tbsp mint extract

• ½ cup sour-cream

• 2 Tbsp flour

• 4 eggs, room-temp

TOPPINGS

• Crushed mint Oreos

• Whipped Cream

• Chocolate Sauce

MISC

• Non-stick cooking spray

• Aluminum foil

To Prepare:

1) In a mixing bowl, combine crushed Oreo and melted butter, mix-well.

2) Spray an 8" spring form pan with non-stick cooking spray. Spread Oreo evenly across bottom of pan, then place in the freezer for at least 10 minutes.

3) In a mixing bowl, mix cream cheese and sugar until nice and smooth. Slowly blend in mint, sour-cream, and flour. Then mix in your eggs one at a time until fully blended.

4) Pour batter over your crust and cover spring form pan with aluminum foil. Make sure to make a foil sling.

5) Add 2 cups water to pressure pot and lower spring form pan into pot.

6) Close and seal lid. Cook on manual HIGH pressure for 35 minutes. Allow for a 10-minute Natural Pressure Release and Quick Release any remaining steam.

7) Open lid, remove and uncover cheesecake. Let cool in refrigerator for at least 4 hours.

8) Once cheesecake is cooled, go ahead and top your cheesecake with crushed mint Oreos, whipped cream, and chocolate sauce. ENJOY!

Crazy Good
Creme Brulee

Ingredients

- 1 cup heavy whipping cream
- 2 egg yolks
- 1 tsp pure vanilla extract
- 1 ½ Tbsp sugar (plus 2 tsp for caramelizing)
- ½ tsp salt
- Aluminum foil

To Prepare:

1) In a mixing bowl, whisk together egg yolks, pure vanilla, 1 ½ Tbsp sugar, and salt.

2) In a microwave safe bowl or cup, heat heavy whipping cream for 45 seconds.

3) Once done, slowly combine heavy whipping cream with egg yolk mixture, whisking until blended.

4) Evenly pour mixture into ramekins (makes 3) and cover each with aluminum foil.

5) Add 1 cup water and trivet to pressure pot. Place ramekins on trivet.

6) Close and seal lid. Cook on manual HIGH pressure for 7-minutes. Allow for a 5-minute Natural Pressure Release and Quick Release any remaining pressure.

7) Open lid, remove and uncover your Crème Brulee. Allow to refrigerate for at least 4 hours (or up to 3 days) before serving.

8) Once cooled and ready to serve, sprinkle each ramekin with 1-2 tsp of sugar and place in oven to BROIL until caramelized. Top with your favorite fruits or other toppings and ENJOY!

Miscellaneous Goodies

Pure Pressure
Applesauce

Ingredients

- 3lbs apples (core & peeled)
- ¾ cups water
- 1 Tbsp lemon juice
- 1 tsp cinnamon
- ¼ tsp ginger

To Prepare:

1) Place all the ingredients in your pot and close/seal the lid. Cook on manual HIGH pressure for 5 minutes. Allow for pressure to release naturally to avoid hot steaming applesauce!

2) Remove lid and smash/stir the applesauce. SERVE & ENJOY!

Pro Tip: For an extra sweet treat, top with honey, syrup, or MORE cinnamon!

Systematic Strawberry Jam

Ingredients

- 1lb. fresh strawberries (remove hull & chop)
- 1 cup honey
- 1 Tbsp cornstarch

To Prepare:

1) Preheat pressure pot using Sauté mode. Once hot, add 1cup honey and continue to cook until it starts to bubble.

2) Next, add your strawberries to the pot. Once the honey mixture starts to turn a pinkish color, turn off Sauté mode.

3) Close and seal your lid. Cook on manual HIGH pressure for 1 minute. Allow for 10 minutes of Normal Pressure Release. Quick release any remaining pressure.

4) Open lid, whisk in 1 Tbsp cornstarch to the mixture until fully dissolved.

5) Allow your Jam to fully cool before transporting it into any jars to avoid severe burns. Spread on your favorite food items and ENJOY!!

Pure Pressure Cinnamon Apples

Ingredients

- 3 apples
- 1 ½ tsp cinnamon
- 1 ½ tsp maple syrup

To Prepare:

1) Peel, core, and slice the apples.

2) Combine apples, cinnamon, and maple syrup in the pressure pot. Add 3 Tbsp water to the pot and give ingredients a good stir to coat the apples.

3) Cook on manual HIGH pressure for 2 minutes. Quick Release the steam.

4) Serve immediately while warm! ENJOY!

Chunky Home-style Garlic Mashed Potatoes

Ingredients

- 2 1/2 tsp kosher salt
- 2 ½ lbs. Yukon Gold potatoes, peeled and cut into 1-inch chunks
- 1 cup Greek yogurt, room-temp
- 1 Tbsp butter, room-temp
- 1/2 tsp pepper
- 3 Tbsp fresh chives, chopped
- 1/2 Tbsp fresh thyme, chopped
- 1/4 cup grated Parmesan cheese

To Prepare:

1) Add 1 cup water and 2 ½ tsp kosher salt to pressure pot. Add steam basket (see back of book) and place chunks of potatoes inside.

2) Close and seal lid. Cook on manual HIGH pressure for 8 minutes. Quick Release the steam.

3) Open lid and add remaining ingredients. Use a hand mixer to mash potatoes easier.

4) Press sauté mode and stir until warm. Serve with your favorite Pure Pressure meal and ENJOY!

Pure Pressure Fresh Brew ICED TEA

Ingredients

- 2 apples, peeled and quartered.
- 5 tea bags (I use Lipton)
- 6 cups water
- Honey for a sweetener (optional)
- ½ tsp baking soda

To Prepare:

1. Add 6 cups water to your pressure pot and press the sauté mode.

2. Once water starts to come to a simmer, add your remaining ingredients (except for honey) and give it a good stir.

3. Close and seal lid. Cook on manual HIGH pressure for 5 minutes. Quick Release the pressure.

4. Open lid. Strain tea into a large container, adding 1 Tbsp honey at a time (testing in-between), until it reaches desired taste.

5. Refrigerated for a couple hours. Serve over ice with favorite cream. ENJOY!

Super Creamy White Hot- Chocolate

Ingredients

- 3 cups milk
- 1/4 cup Cacao Butter
- 2 ½ Tbsp honey
- 2 tsp pure vanilla extract
- 1/8 tsp sea salt
- 2 Tbsp gelatin powder
- 1 Tbsp butter
- Whipped cream for topping (optional)
- White chocolate sauce/shavings for topping (optional)

To Prepare:

1) Add everything except for the gelatin powder to your pressure pot and give it a good stir.

2) Close and seal lid. Cook on manual LOW pressure for 6 minutes and then Quick Release the pressure when done.

3) Open the lid and pour your Hot Chocolate into a blender, adding gelatin powder. (Make sure to leave at least 3 inches in your blender as the Hot Chocolate will foam)

4) Top with whipped cream and white chocolate sauce/shavings. ENJOY!

Pure Addiction Caramel Corn

Ingredients

- ½ cup popping corn
- 2 tsp coconut oil
- 5 Tbsp butter
- ¼ cup sugar
- ½ cup milk

To Prepare:

1) Press sauté mode on your pressure cooker. When hot, add 2 tsp coconut oil and 2 ½ Tbsp butter (half). Cook until fully melted.

2) Once melted, add in popping corn and mix-well.

3) Press the adjust on the sauté function and this will bring the temperature up to hot.

4) Wait until it starts popping and then place the lid on top of your pressure cooker and wait until it has not popped for 2-3 minutes.

5) While the corn is popping make your caramel sauce. Add your sugar into a saucepan along with 2 tsp water. Place it on a medium heat and leave until it starts going light brown. (DO NOT mix, this will crystalize it) Once it goes light brown, add your butter.

6) When the butter has melted, mix it in and turn the heat down to low. Then, gradually add your milk until the sauce coats the back of your spoon. Set aside to cool.

7) Empty popcorn from pressure pot into a mixing/serving bowl. Pour caramel sauce over top (save some) and "toss" popcorn until everything is covered.

8) Place in the fridge for about an hour and then toss in sauce one final time to give it that true caramel corn crunch. Serve and ENJOY!

Crave-able Chicken Gravy

Ingredients

Starter

- 1lb chicken wings
- 1 large onion, quartered
- 1 carrot, chunked
- 3 cloves of garlic, minced
- 1 Bay leaves
- 2 stems rosemary
- 2 sprigs fresh sage
- 2 stems of fresh thyme
- 1 tsp sea salt
- 1 tsp pepper
- 1 tsp ground allspice

To finish

- 4 Tbsp corn flour
- 1 Tbsp Marsala wine
- Extra seasoning (optional)

To Prepare:

1) Pop bones out of middle of chicken wings and then chop wings into 2-3 chunks. (You need to expose bone marrow to thicken your gravy)

2) Press sauté mode on your pressure cooker. When hot, add all your "starter" ingredients, except for the allspice. Continue to cook until all chicken wings are nice and browned.

3) Turn of sauté mode. Add 4 ¼ cups cold water to your ingredients and give it a good stir.

4) Close and seal lid. Cook on manual HIGH pressure for 45 minutes. Allow for a 10-minute Natural Pressure Release and then Quick Release any remaining steam.

5) Open lid and strain stock into a large bowl. Clean out your pressure pot. Then, hit sauté mode and pour your stock back into the pot.

6) Whisk together corn flour and 4 Tbsp of cold water in a small bowl. (If needed, use a little bit of hot stock to break up lumps)

7) When the stock starts to bubble in the pressure pot, pour in enough of the corn flour mixture to thicken to desired texture. Whisk constantly! (Stir in corn flour very slow as it will thicken quickly)

8) Stir in Marsala wine and taste the gravy for seasoning - add further salt and pepper if desired.

9) Keep gravy on warm to serve over your favorite food! ENJOY!

**PRO TIP: Freeze leftover gravy in zip-lock bags. Thaw it out the night before for a mess-free homemade chicken gravy that everyone will crave!

Pure Pressure
BUBBLE TEA

Ingredients

• 1 ½ cups Tapioca or "Boba" pearls (I use WuFuYuan, the cheap ones turn mushy)

• 1 cup ice (plus extra for ice bath)

• 1 cup milk

• 2 scoops vanilla ice cream

• Taro or "Boba" powder to flavor (optional)

To Prepare:

1) Add Tapioca peals and 1 ½ cups water to pressure pot.

2) Close and seal lid. Use your "bean/chili" mode and cook for 1 minute, then Quick Release any pressure.

3) Open lid and drain Tapioca pearls. Put them in a cold ice bath right away and give it a stir.

4) Scoop out 3 Tbsp of Tapioca pearls (per serving) and place into a drinking glass.

5) Add in 1 cup ice, 1 cup milk, and 2 scoops vanilla ice-cream. Give it a good stir. Use a big straw to enjoy true Bubble Tea flavor. ENJOY!

Pure Pressure Classic Hummus

Ingredients

Beans

- ½ lb. dry garbanzo beans
- 1/2 tsp garlic powder
- 1/2 tsp salt

Hummus

- drained, cooked garbanzo beans
- 3/4 cup reserved cooking liquid
- 1/3 cup tahini
- ½ lemon, zested
- 1 lemon, juiced
- 2 Tbsp olive oil
- 3/4 tsp salt
- 1/4 tsp pepper
- 1/4 tsp cumin
- 1 tsp garlic powder
- Oregano, Parsley, Olive Oil, or any other favorite topping!

To Prepare:

Beans

1) Add the water, dry beans, garlic powder and salt to your pressure pot.

2) Close and seal lid. Cook on manual HIGH pressure for 60 minutes. Allow for a FULL Natural Pressure Release. (Takes about 15 minutes or so)

3) Open lid and drain beans. (make sure to reserve your ¾ cup of cooking liquid)

Hummus

4) Once the beans have slightly cooled, add about half cup of cooking liquid (for starting out), tahini, lemon zest, lemon juice, olive oil, salt, pepper and cumin to a food processor or blender.

5) Stop the food processor/blender and check the taste and consistency. Add more cooking liquid, if desired. (I used the full ¾ cup)

6) Can be refrigerated for 1 week. Serve with toasty pita, chips, veggies and ENJOY!!

Awesome Apple Butter

Ingredients

- 5 – 6 apples (I used Fuji)
- ¼ cup apple cider
- 1 cup light brown sugar
- 2 tsp apple pie spice
- ½ tsp salt
- 1 cinnamon stick
- 1 tsp pure vanilla extract

To Prepare:

1) Place all the ingredients into the pressure pot.

2) Close and seal lid. Cook on manual HIGH pressure for 8 minutes. Allow for a 10-minute Natural Pressure Release and Quick Release any remaining steam.

3) Open lid and remove cinnamon stick.

4) Pour apple mixture into a food processor/blender to puree.

5) Turn pressure cook back on sauté mode. Pour apple mixture back into pressure pot and stir continuously for 10-15 minutes until desired thickness.

6) Cool completely.

7) Transfer to a glass jar. Cover and refrigerate for up to 3 weeks or freeze in small containers up to 3 months. ENJOY!!

Outstanding Orange Marmalade

Ingredients

- 3lbs oranges
- 4 lbs. sugar
- 1 cup water (for mixing)
- 3-4 canning jars
- Thermometer

To Prepare:

1) Wash and finely slice your oranges. (Make sure to save the juices)

2) Add 1 cup water and oranges to pressure pot.

3) Close and seal lid. Cook on manual HIGH minutes for 10 minutes. Allow for a 10-minute Natural Pressure Release and Quick Release any remaining. (Prep canning jars while cooking)

4) Open lid and stir in sugar. Press sauté mode and continue stirring until it reaches a temperature of 223 degrees. (Marmalade should be "jiggly" if you scoop a spoonful)

5) Allow to cool for at least 15 minutes before serving. Also, lasts several weeks refrigerated in canning jars. ENJOY!

Right Off the Vine Red Wine

Ingredients

• Grape Juice (64oz bottle, I used Welch's)

• 1 cup sugar (granulated)

• a funnel

• 1 pack Red Wine Yeast (OR White Wine Yeast)

• Pressure Cooker WITH Yogurt Function

• Clear boxing tape

To Prepare:

1) Open your grape juice and remove 1 cup to set aside. Add your 1 cup sugar to the bottle of opened juice and then put cap back on. Shake continuously for 1-2 minutes until fully dissolved.

2) Now open your grape juice again and add ½ packet of Red Wine yeast. Replace cap and continue to shake again until dissolved.

3) Once dissolved, dump bottle in your pressure pot along with the 1 cup of grape juice you previously set aside. (Save juice bottle for later)

4) Close lid but DO NOT seal vent. (Needs to breathe) Press the "Yogurt" function, and then press less. You MUST press LESS to allow the yeast to do its thing.

5) Now you need to have some patience!! You're going to run the time for a total of 48 hours!! Each day, let it run for 24 hours.

6) In step 4, you will notice that I said DO NOT seal the vent on your lid. The reason is that this is your starting point. Every 6-8 hours, you want to alternate opening the lid vent and closing the lid vent. So, for the first round, you will leave the vent open. Wait 6-8 hours (depending if you're sleeping or not!), and then close the vent. Then alternate

7) After your 48 hours is up, you can transfer the wine "juice" back into your plastic container.

Take the plastic lid and place it on HALF way. You don't want it to seal tight. (Pressure will build up and blow the lid off your bottle and leave you with a nice mess!)

8) Secure the plastic cap on the bottle with the clear packing tape. Place a piece of tape across, and then place a piece of tape around the neck to keep the tape in place.

9) Allow wine to sit in a cool-dark place until all the fizziness has gone away (Mine took about 8 days, but remember, the longer the better!) Drink with friends! ENJOY!

Electrifying Elderberry Syrup

Ingredients

- ¾ cup organic dried elderberries
- 1 cinnamon stick
- 1 chunk fresh ginger
- 1/2 tsp clove powder
- 4 cups filtered water
- 1 cup raw honey
- 3-4 canning jars

To Prepare:

1) Add everything EXCEPT for the honey into your pressure pot.

2) Close and seal lid. Cook on manual HIGH pressure for 7 minutes. Quick Release the pressure.

3) Open lid and press sauté mode. Stir in honey.

4) Continue to cook and stir for about 15-minutes until syrup has thickened. Pour into canning jars and wait at least 15-minutes before serving. BOOST THAT IMMUNE SYSTEM AND ENJOY!!

**PRO TIP: Heat ¼ Elderberry Syrup, ¾ cup apple juice, and 3 packs plain gelatin on stovetop until dissolved and transfer to your favorite gummy bear mold to cool for a healthy treat to boost your families Immune Systems!

Muy Bien Mexican Rice

Ingredients

- 2 tsp oil
- ¼ cup onion, chopped
- ½ cups instant white rice (I use Minute Rice)
- 1 cup chicken broth
- 1 cup salsa

To Prepare:

1) Heat the oil in a large skillet over medium-high heat. Add the onion and sauté for about 2-3 minutes.

2) Add the instant rice into the skillet and sauté for an additional 1-2 minutes.

3) Add the chicken broth and salsa to the rice and stir well to combine.

4) Bring the mixture to a boil and remove from the heat. Cover with a lid and set aside until all the liquid has absorbed, about 5-7 minutes.

5) Serve with your favorite Pure Pressure meal and ENJOY!

Sugary Candy Pecans

Ingredients

- 4 cups pecan halves
- 2/3 cup pure maple syrup
- 1/2 tbsp pure vanilla extract
- 1/2 tbsp cinnamon
- 1/2 tsp nutmeg
- 1/2 tsp salt
- ½ cup sugar
- ½ cup brown sugar

To Prepare:

1) Press sauté on your pressure cooker. Add pecans, syrup, vanilla, cinnamon, nutmeg, and salt. Sauté ingredients until pecans are tender (about 5-10 minutes). Make sure to stir consistently so nothing burns.

2) When pecans are tender, turn pressure cooker off. Add 1/2 cup of water. Close and seal lid. Cook on manual HIGH pressure for 10 minutes. (Preheat oven to 375 degrees when cooking) Quick Release the pressure when done.

3) Open lid and pour mixture onto a baking sheet in a single layer. Bake in preheated oven for 5 minutes, then flip pecans. Place pecans back in the oven for another 5 minutes.

4) In a mixing bowl, whisk together ½ cup sugar and ½ cup brown sugar. Allow pecans to cool at least 5-minutes and then toss in sugar. Bag them up and ENJOY!!

Pure Pressure Yummy Yogurts

Ingredients

• 1 Tbsp plain Greek yogurt (with active cultures)

• 1 (52oz.) bottle of ultra-filtered whole milk (I use Fair Life)

• 1 (14oz) can of sweetened condensed milk

• Favorite toppings

• Pressure cooker MUST have Yogurt function

To Prepare:

1) In your pressure pot, whisk together whole milk and sweetened condensed milk until slightly foamy.

2) Close lid. (no need to seal) Press "Yogurt" and set for 8 hours. When finished remove pressure pot from cooker and cover with aluminum foil.

3) Allow to sit in refrigerator for at least an additional 4 hours. Then add your favorite toppings and ENJOY!!

Pure Pressure Products

www.purepressurecooking.com

1.   6" & 8" Round Cheesecake Push Pan
2.   Silicone Non-Stick Whisk
3.   Silicone Non-Scratch Steam Basket
4.   Silicone Anti-Slip Cooking Glove
5.   7" Non-Stick Springform Cheesecake Pan
6.   Stainless Steel Expandable Steamer Basket
7.   Heat Resistant Silicone Egg Bite/Muffin Pan
8.   Elevated Egg/Steam Rack
9.   Silicone Non-Slip Cooking Grips
10.   3pk Silicone Seal Rings
11.   Silicone Cooking Squares 4 & 9 Cavity

First Printing: 2018

ISBN 978-1-387-59437-5

Pure Pressure Cooking

Hoffman St

Three Rivers, Michigan 49093

www.PurePressureCooking.com

31337784R00083

Made in the USA
Lexington, KY
18 February 2019